Develop Your Psychic Skills

Develop your
PSYCHIC
SKILLS

by Enid Hoffman

Schiffer Publishing Ltd ®

4880 Lower Valley Road Atglen, pennsylvania 19310

This book is dedicated to Aunt Lizzie and Uncle Walter

Library of Congress Control Number: 2014946601

Typesetting by Betty Bauman
Edited by Jane Graham and Jeanne Leone

ISBN: 978-0-914918-29-5
Printed in China

Published by Schiffer Publishing, Ltd.
4880 Lower Valley Road
Atglen, PA 19310
Phone: (610) 593-1777; Fax: (610) 593-2002
E-mail: Info@schifferbooks.com

Contents

Introduction

Do you want to go through life only half alive? Most of us use only half of the brain we were born with, the left hemisphere, with its logical, analytical and rational functions. This book will help you develop the powers of the *primary* brain of the other hemisphere, the brain of "first impressions," intuition and feelings. Lightning fast, it registers information beyond reach of our normal conscious perception—hence the common belief that "your first impression is usually right." The right brain "knows," the left brain "guesses" and theorizes.

Rather than live out your life in uncertainty, guessing at answers, develop your psychic skills and enjoy the wonderful sensation of being *sure* and knowing the true reality that exists behind and within objective facts.

Students in psychic development are often counselled to follow first impressions. Why? Because your first impression comes from your "primary brain," the right hemisphere, the seat of the intuitive powers so few of us use or develop. Guesses, theories, rationalizations—these come from the logical left hemisphere, the "secondary" brain of second thoughts and afterthoughts, the seat of so-called ordinary states of consciousness where we function nearly all our lives.

By developing your natural inborn psychic senses you will open up entirely new avenues of communication with others. You will "see" people differently, sensing what is going on inside them. You will begin to sense the vital energies of thoughts and feelings flowing in and around people, invisible and inaudible to our physical senses. You will be able to intuit what someone will say next, and to respond to what is really going on instead of what appears to be happening.

With the insight and foreknowledge that this new power will give you, you will be able to look within, when in doubt, and see what lies ahead. You can tap this pool of inner knowledge easily and effortlessly. Superconsciousness: it is right there, behind and hidden by "normal" consciousness.

It took me years to appreciate my psychic gifts, to see how my flashes of inspiration paid off as I followed my hunches. As my skills got sharper, I realized that I had an edge over others. I began to rely more and more on inner senses that I had previously ignored.

All too often we live in homes, offices and factories that are so logical, regimented and mechanical that we lose touch with our inner knowledge. Rational, intellectual thought takes precedence over our feelings about how things should be. Life becomes boring, dull and repetitious.

People and life have new meaning and purpose when you can look into them instead of merely glancing at their surfaces. People will *come alive* for you in an intimate and unifying way when you learn to see beyond their outer shells. Instead of the formal conventions that are the norm of behavior, you will be able to participate with spontaneous and natural responses to what is really going on now.

With your expanded perception and your ability to create new situations, you will be a more effective person, more alive and exciting to yourself and others. The time and energy you put into the practices offered in this book will have many payoffs, both in terms of your own life experience, and your opportunities to enhance the experiences of others. As you progress beyond the usual ways of exercising your abilities, you will move into new dimensions of consciousness and awareness, where living becomes increasingly exciting and new. Your psychic skills will magnetically attract the fulfillment of your needs and desires, easily.

Doing the experiments in this book will activate your intuitional brain. The experience of "knowing" that you are correct before the "evidence" is in will become more familiar to you as you practice, demonstrating that your psychic skills are becoming stronger.

As the psychologist and inner-space explorer John Lilly has said, your only limits are your beliefs. If you hold contradictory beliefs, as most of us do, your life will be filled with conflict. By using techniques explained in this book, you can begin resolving the inner contradictions that produce conflict in your life; you can begin eliminating the negative beliefs about your psychic skills, about yourself and about the world, that are holding you back.

This book offers you a wide choice of activities and exercises, and solid explanations of how and why your psychic skills work. You can have an exciting evening with your friends recalling past lives, or learning to sense color with your eyes shut. You can learn to see auras and sense the subtle manifestations of vital energies.

The practices offered here are fun, especially for groups of people. In many ways you may get faster results or easier progress if you work in a group. Many years of experience by myself and others have verified that these practices work. That is why this book is especially good as a text for psychic development classes.

There are many ways to use the book. You can read through it completely, systematically, or skip over the detailed instructions for any given experiment until you decide to use it. If you want to get right to the nitty-gritty you might want to skip the first chapter with its autobiographical detail—but watch out: it too contains some steps in developing your psychic skills!

This book is a broad overview of the whole field of psychic expertise. You can use it to develop your skills for your own satisfaction, to demonstrate their validity to others, or to help others. As you develop your psychic skills, a wider range of choices will open to you. Become a healer. Know what others are doing and thinking. See what the future holds for you and others. Make your relationships more intimate and meaningful. Re-create your lifestyle to allow space for all your feelings to be expressed in positive ways. Take your choice. Or do all of them. Whatever your preference, there is something for you.

It is now up to you.

1

How I Developed My Psychic Skills

I have always felt it important for my students to understand how natural and human a process it is to develop one's psychic skills. Although some events in this process may seem strange or "spooky," it is not necessary to surround them with an aura of awe and mystery in order to believe in them. One object of this book, as I have said in the Introduction, is to help you realize how your psychic abilities are as "normal" as your physical eyesight and hearing.

For this reason, I want to tell you in this chapter some of the story of how I developed my psychic skills. I had the help of many friends and teachers, both in the body and discarnate.

I have dedicated this book to my Aunt Lizzie not only because she introduced me to the world of psychic phenomena, but also because she lavished so much love and caring on me during my childhood.

I'd like you to see her as I saw her then. A bird-like little woman, with erect posture and her feet solidly planted on the ground, she bustled about taking care of her practical day-to-day responsibilities as the wife of my Uncle Walter. Uncle Walter was a big bear of a man who spoiled me with gentle smiles and nickels for ice cream cones as Aunt Lizzie clucked her disapproval. We both adored him.

Of my father's three sisters, it was Aunt Lizzie who "adopted" me as her favorite niece. I spent many summers of my childhood in her Vermont home. Often Aunt Lizzie and Uncle Walter took me on their trips selling real estate, and on excursions to the country to pick blueberries or visit relatives.

I vividly remember standing by their low sink one morning, Uncle Walter awkwardly brushing my hair, Aunt Lizzie bustling about preparing breakfast. That memory comes to me with all the warmth of their kitchen and the wonderful odors of bacon frying and coffee brewing.

As other interests beckoned in my teens, my close relationship with Aunt Lizzie lapsed. We had little contact until I was in my early twenties, married and busy being a housewife and mother.

Uncle Walter had been dead a number of years, and Aunt Lizzie had turned to spiritualism to continue her relationship with him. She was a member of a small group which met weekly to communicate with those "on the other side of life," as they phrased it.

Spiritualism affirms that there is communication between the so-called dead and the living, and spiritualists work with that affirmation in a very concrete way. In circle sittings and seances they communicate and receive messages through mental mediumship, automatic writing and various other kinds of channeling. My aunt was able to do automatic writing during these sittings, and Uncle Walter guided her hand as she held the pencil poised over blank paper. He wrote her letters of love and guidance.

Aunt Lizzie also learned to energize a table with a circle of people around it, so that the table communicated messages in response to questions from the sitters. This was called "table tilting." When I participated the table lifted off the floor on two legs and came down with a thump.

When Aunt Lizzie told me of her interest and activities I became curious. It was Aunt Lizzie who introduced me to my first seance.

Follow me and imagine the event. My eldest son was then two years old, and accompanied us on the short walk down Western Avenue to the home of one of the circle members. We were welcomed into a gracious home where we joined four women in the living room. All of us gathered around the piano and sang hymns. I was told they did this to lift their consciousness to higher levels, and to provide protection from low-level spirits. I don't remember my son David singing, but he was at ease with the group as he held my hand.

In a darkened dining room we sat around a heavy oak table. David was curled in my lap, quiet but watchful. The silence pervading the room deepened as we all relaxed expectantly, waiting for something to happen.

In front of Aunt Lizzie was a stack of blank paper. Pencils lay alongside the paper. Another woman had a similar stack of paper and pencils. In the dim light I saw Aunt Lizzie and her friend pick up the pencils and poise them over the top sheet of paper. For the next fifteen minutes or so the only sound to break the silence was the scratching of pencils.

Slowly I became aware that the writing had ceased. A quiet discussion began among the women. The lights were turned on and we realized that the seance was over.

Now came the reading of what was written. Most of Aunt Lizzie's was from Walter, advising her on mundane affairs. As always, Uncle Walter included expressions of his continued love and caring. The other woman received messages from her dead relatives too, but she also received some philosophical remarks purportedly from "spirit teachers" who were teaching the group at its weekly meetings.

I listened politely, but was quite skeptical about the happenings of the seance. Up until that moment I had no time for things of this nature. Now my curiosity was piqued, and I was keen to learn more about psychic phenomena. I decided then and there to pursue knowledge of other worlds, other realities, the occult and esoteric, and to develop my own psychic skills. My interest has never flagged.

I soon had an opportunity to continue my new studies. Aunt Lizzie and I were visiting my sister Joy and decided to hold a "table tilting" seance. Others were invited over for the evening. The plans were made. Joy and I had our children tucked safely away upstairs. Our friends gathered in the living room with Aunt Lizzie and the time arrived to begin.

Let your imagination help you to visualize the event and "be there" with us. The living room was dark. One small lamp furnished a faint glow for the group circling a large, low, oak coffee table in the center of the room. Hands, barely visible in the dim light, were poised delicately over the tabletop, palms downward, fingertips just touching the surface, the beginning of the seance. All was quiet. Nothing was happening yet.

Aunt Lizzie began by explaining to us some of the features we could expect to occur, as she invited the spirits of relatives and teachers to communicate with us. We waited. Some of us were nervous, others skeptical, some relaxed and expectant. The table began to vibrate. We all felt it. Aunt Lizzie inquired, "Is someone here who would like to communicate? If so, two raps for yes and one rap for no."

Immediately the table rose up on two legs and came down with a thump. The table rose again and came down with a thump. Aunt Lizzie took that to mean yes. From then on, each one of us volunteered questions, sometimes all talking at once. The table vibrated and thumped. Slowly and methodically we determined that the communicators were people who had lived in this house previously. We kept asking them questions until the table refused to move, about two hours later. Then we turned on lights and had coffee while we discussed what had happened during the evening. You may imagine how fascinated I was by all of this, and how delighted I was to share it with my sister.

My visits to table-tipping seances were sporadic. I was a busy mother with little time to spare for people who did not inhabit my physical world. However, my curiosity led me to literature on spiritualism, and soon occult books became my favorite reading matter. The public library proved a limited source for these, so I began to build the library I now possess.

After all of my children were in school and well on their way to adulthood, my search for knowledge of occult things began in earnest. Whenever I got a chance, I plied Aunt Lizzie with questions, and she willingly shared with me what she had experienced. She gave me the privilege of reading some of the philosophical material she had received through automatic writing, as well as some of her personal messages from Uncle Walter. Through her, I learned of other paranormal phenomena that still remain unexplained by the scientific community.

Some of these paranormal phenomena I witnessed while visiting Aunt Lizzie. One morning I asked Aunt Lizzie if I could help her fix breakfast in her sunny kitchen. She assigned me the task of making toast in her old-fashioned toaster. This contraption had two sides with an exposed coil between. I let each side down by hand, placed bread on them and then pushed them upright to toast the bread against the glowing coil which filled the center section. I watched the toaster reach an orange glow. Standing there, watching the bread toast, I saw the coil suddenly change from bright cherry red to black. "Aunt Lizzie! Something's wrong! The toaster just stopped!" Her response was the familiar clucking sound I had heard so often, and she spoke. "Uncle Walter, you turn that right back on and stop being mischievous!" To my amazement the coil reddened at once and stayed that way.

That day she told me tales of how Uncle Walter affected electrical appliances in her apartment, turning lights on and off, stopping electric clocks, and now the toaster. These were common pastimes for Uncle Walter. I had no way to verify these stories, but I respected her belief because I knew her to be a down-to-earth, truthful, intelligent person. I was still only half-convinced, however. I needed a personal experience to validate her ideas for myself. It would be a long time before I really believed in a life after death or the reality of psychic phenomena.

Around 1962, Aunt Lizzie interested my husband Bill in spiritualism, which led us to attend a church service in Stamford, Connecticut to hear a sermon by Arthur Ford. By that time, Ford had attained national fame as a medium. His topic was the founding of the Spiritual Frontiers Fellowship, an organization, still in existence, whose purpose is to investigate, study and discuss psychic phenomena as they occur in historical Christianity.

After the service, Reverend Raymond Burns, the minister of the church, was at the rear, shaking hands with each departing individual as we filed out with the rest of the congregation. A kindly-looking grey-haired gentleman, he greeted us and made us feel welcome. When my husband spoke of our interest in joining his "psychic development" class, he hesitated only a moment before inviting us to join the Friday evening group.

Gathered with twenty other students in the outer auditorium the following Friday evening, we heard Reverend Burns welcome us all and give a brief prayer as we sat quietly. Then we all rose and followed him into a room directly behind the auditorium. This was a special room used only for seances and classes, completely dark when the door was closed. Reverend Burns switched on a small lamp, and the rosy glow from its red bulb allowed us to move about and find seats. Someone closed the door and Reverend Burns switched off the lamp. Total darkness enveloped us. I was awed, a little scared, and very nervous, but I tried to relax. I had no idea what to expect.

Soon an unfamiliar voice issued from Reverend Burns. The voice introduced itself as a teacher, and gave a short talk. Then Reverend Burns came out of his self-induced trance and spoke briefly in his normal voice. For nearly two hours voices of different spirit teachers addressed their individual students through Reverend Burns. A new teacher introduced himself to me and my husband, greeting us and warmly welcoming us to the series of seances we would attend to develop our psychic abilities.

The hour's drive home was filled with our excitement over what had occurred, and what might yet occur as we pursued this new endeavor.

Gradually, week by week, we became better able to receive ideas telepathically from our teachers, and to report what we had received when our turn came in class. With each class our skills improved. Gradually my guesses turned into accurate responses. I didn't really notice the point at which I became convinced at last of the reality of unseen spirits and psychic phenomena.

Now my search for more information and greater skill in the arts of psychic perception and projection was on in earnest. I joined many groups, worked under the tutelage of others through the mail and took lessons to improve my understanding and my psychic talents. I became able to give psychic readings and to recall past lives. I had a few spontaneous experiences of psychic phenomena. When my studies in psychology revealed how suggestible people are, I ceased giving psychic readings and turned to sharing what I knew and had learned, so that others would develop their own psychic skills and get their information straight from the source, so to speak. I continued reading about psychics, mediums and others who were able to perform psychic feats far greater than mine.

I was very fortunate to find a class in psychic development that was of very high caliber. These are few and far between. The majority of people who want to develop their psychic skills cannot find anything like it. Over the years I have explored many paths which have turned out to be dead ends for me. Out of this experience I have resolved to create methods which are easy and safe, and yet powerful, productive and beneficial.

The theories which I have developed have been tested on myself and others. I have participated in many experiments and shared in the experiences of the other participants. Many people have shared with me their problems and their successes in developing their abilities. Out of all of this I learned to help others develop their psychic skills successfully.

Now I have organized what I learned and experienced, and have set it forth in this book. Be aware of me as the author, supporting you in your efforts as I do with each individual in my classes, in person. Use your imagination to sense my presence, and receive my loving desire that you grow and expand, using your psychic skills to make your world a better place to live in.

It may surprise you to learn that you have already been practicing your psychic skills as you read this chapter. The power of your imagination enabled you to visualize and inwardly experience the people and scenes I have described. You have already begun to develop your psychic powers by establishing this rapport with me and my personal history.

As you use and strengthen your imaginative skills in the experiments and exercises that follow, you will progress further and faster than you might presently believe. Be prepared to change some beliefs, beliefs that you may not even have been aware of holding. Enjoy your progress. Have a lot of fun with these practices, and step by tiny step you will move toward that moment when, in response to some casual remark you make, someone will cry out "you must be psychic!"

2

We All Have Psychic Skills

At one time or another everyone has had a hunch which has paid off. The phone rings, but *before* you answer it you already know who it is. You go to your mail box and know *ahead of time* that a letter from a particular person will be there waiting for you. You see a stranger on a street and know that that unknown person will somehow be important in your life. These are all examples of psychic happenings. Locked within each of us lies the power to expand our consciousness beyond our present awareness. For want of a better term, this power is called "psychic ability." Everyone has it. Few know how to use it or how to command it. Like most people, you may be aware of your ability to perceive things beyond the level of the accepted five senses, sight, sound, touch, smell and taste, but unlike most people you are about to learn to awaken this ability and develop your psychic skills.

How to get at these psychic abilities has long been considered mysterious. Popular opinion holds that some people, the lucky ones, are born with "the gift." These lucky people come equipped with psychic abilities. The truth of the matter is that these people have enough awareness of their hunches to take the time to develop this ability, in much the same way people develop their intellect, their athletic competence, and so on, one step at a time. Everyone has the ability to think; no one would argue with that. But it is evident that some people are able to think better than others. This is not so much a matter of native ability as it is of *training* that native ability to get the most out of it. It is from this premise that I have taken the liberty to term these so-called psychic gifts, *skills*. It is my belief that anyone, with a little practice, can develop psychic skills.

Psychic skills can be developed in the same manner as a person learns to swim. If you throw a nonswimmer into the water, the person may learn to swim, may drown, or may simply splash to shore and safety. The sink-or-swim way is a nondirected approach to learning, which leaves the method as well as the responsibility with the learner. If, on the other hand, you provide swimming lessons (the directed approach), the person not only learns to swim in a nonthreatening environment, but also learns a variety of swimming strokes as well. The new swimmer learns to be comfortable in the water, and to feel personal power in a new environment.

Developing psychic skills is exactly like learning to swim. It is learning to function well in a different environment, the psychic environment. With the sink-or-swim method, a person might learn to develop psychic skills, but just as easily might "drown" or merely "splash ashore and to safety." With a disciplined, systematic approach a person will learn through study to develop a wider, more reliable repertoire of skills for coping with the psychic environment. The development of all skills follows a similar pattern. First we observe, then imitate, then practice. With practice, we achieve the level of competence that was our goal.

As children, we saw other people walk, jump and skip. We began to imitate, awkwardly at first, but with practice and after many failures we were soon able to walk, jump and skip proudly. Certainly it never occurred to us to quit walking; we just kept with it until we had it right. Later we moved on to greater challenges like riding a tricycle, and then a two-wheeler. As we grew older, we learned other things, through the same routine.

Learning physical skills was paralleled by learning the mental skills taught in school. There we learned to memorize, to concentrate, to pay attention long enough to understand. We learned to think and to work out problems.

Remember the days when you first learned to drive a car. You had to be shown each procedure in order to become an accomplished driver. Consciously performing each step in sequence, you gradually memorized them until you began to perform them automatically, through your inner self, which absorbs the routine.

In each case the process was the same. First, there was the awareness that the goal was within the realm of possibility. Anyone can ride a bike or drive a car. Why should I be different? If they can, I can. Next came the commitment to acquire the skill. I *will* learn to drive the car. Then came the preparation to make the skill yours. Either you watched someone else who was accomplished, and tried to imitate that person's behavior, or you found someone who could show you how to do it. Then you practiced. Reflect a moment on the skills you have. Can you type? Do you remember learning the keyboard? Remember practicing hour after hour? You kept at it, because this was a skill you wanted. You counted the errors and then went back and typed the page again. There were fewer errors and finally almost none. How about learning to hit a ball? First you were terrible; you missed most of the pitches; then your eye got a little better and with each practice session you developed more and more skill.

Developing psychic skills follows the same path. First there is the commitment, then the instruction and finally the practice. It takes patience and perseverance in large quantities. Everyone can develop psychic skills, just as everyone can learn to ride a bike, type or hit a ball. Some will find it easier than others. The rate at which each of us learns is a very personal thing. We must not compare ourselves to others. Just because someone learns faster doesn't necessarily mean he or she learns better. Both the tortoise and the hare get there.

You may ask, "Why should I want to develop my psychic skills?" We develop our psychic skills for the same reason that we develop any other skill—because they enhance our lives. Psychic skills add a dimension you never enjoyed before. They bring increased power over your own circumstances, increased joy in living every day. They assist you in creating your own future, in doing many things that were never in the realm (your version) of the possible or probable.

My purpose is to help you enhance your intuition, your psychic abilities, so that you can improve your life and add to the lives of others. As with any skill, performing psychic feats simply to impress others should be avoided. When you perform your newly learned ability, do it with discretion. With the development of psychic skills comes power, and with power comes responsibility. Our personal power enables us to control our own lives. It is not to control others. We can show others how to control themselves, but we should·not do it for them. We are responsible for ourselves only, and no matter how well intentioned we may be, we have a responsibility not to interfere with anyone else's life design. This is the responsibility of power.

Our Two Selves and Three Minds

In you are two selves. One is *you*, the director, the teacher, the guide, the outer self. The other is the inner self, the worker, the student, the performer of skills. These selves are known by many names—the conscious and the subconscious, the id and the ego. The labels can be important because we want to use names we can identify with. I like to use the word *self* because it means more to me in actual practice than phrases such as "me and my mind." Mind has an impersonal sound to it, as if it were separate from me.

My outer self is that part of me that evaluates, reasons, calculates and uses logic. My inner self is that part of me that records all that happens to me and responds automatically, without judging.

My inner self is like my child, and I am like her parent. She is my student whom I teach, and my accomplished worker who performs for me when taught. I control my inner self, and she accepts my direction and orders willingly. The most important aspect of this inner self is her independence. She functions outside my awareness and is quite different in nature from me. We will consider these differences as we develop our psychic skills: awareness of them will enable us to develop much more efficiently than we would if we were to ignore them.

The inner self perceives and learns differently from the outer self. We teach ourselves each step until it is committed to memory. Repetition of suggestions is the process. We will be using the same technique in developing psychic skills.

The inner self is limited only by our conscious beliefs about it. If we make a conscious decision that we cannot do something, the inner self accepts that decision and makes it a reality. The converse is also true. If we make a conscious decision that we can do something, the inner self accepts the decision and does all in its power to make that decision materialize. And her power is considerable. For example, if you tell yourself that you cannot play the piano, then of course you can't. If, on the other hand, you tell yourself that you can, although you won't sound like Van Cliburn the first time you pick out a tune, the likelihood that you will attain some mastery over the instrument is enhanced. You will find that, if you decide that you would like to play, you will be able to after some practice. By believing that you can master the piano you won't have any negative beliefs getting in the way of your goal. We accept limitations of our inner self as a matter of course. We must review these limitations and begin to reject those that are not valid.

These beliefs can be extended and widened to encompass much more that we thought possible before. We must guard against saying that we cannot do something just because we haven't done it before. If we've tried something and it hasn't worked, it doesn't mean that we cannot do it, only that it needs more work. Watching others who are more proficient at a skill that we wish to acquire is a great way to learn. The ability to mimic, an inherent aspect of the inner self, can be used to develop skills. The other two ways are through instruction and experimentation.

Before we get to the skills themselves, see clearly your two selves which will be working together from now on as a team. Call it "you and your psyche" or "you and your soul." It doesn't matter; but we will use, for convenience, "you and your inner self."

There are three levels of mind operative in your inner self: literal mind, programmed mind and intuitional mind. The *literal mind* is related to the objective world, the world of matter and physical existence. Contents of our literal mind come through our physical senses. We see, hear, taste, smell and touch the world around us. The sensory information registers on the substance of our bodies. The literal mind is the intelligent substance that holds the record of all our experiences. This level of mind or intelligence is always at the base of all other levels. It is real and concrete. It is the world of facts.

The *programmed mind* is the subconscious level where your beliefs dwell. It is here that values are placed on the objective world. This is right, that is wrong. This is a virtue, that is a sin. Beautiful and ugly and all other classifications of this type are in the programmed mind. They develop over the years, moving from your conscious self into the sub-conscious to reside there as a framework for action and behavior. This level of consciousness lies directly above the literal mind and influences all we do. It limits yet allows for expansion. This programmed mind is like a computer, filled from outside ourselves as we grow up, programmed into us by our parents, our teachers and our peers. These are the cultural values; the societal standards that enable us to survive the culture in which we are born. This level of mind is essential to our social survival.

The *intuitional mind* is based on feeling. It is more powerful than the programmed mind. We absorb many concepts that are in conflict with one another and we rely on the intuitional mind, or "gut feeling" to make the appropriate decisions about them.

The intuitional mind lies beyond consciousness, and many of us have blocked its messages meant for the rational, conscious mind. We have been taught to ignore our inner feelings in order to behave and think as others would like us to. Becoming open to the messages from our intuitional mind is very important in the practice of our psychic skills.

The intuitional mind resides in the right hemisphere of our brain. The rational mind sits in the left, where our consciousness is placed. Just below these two is the programmed mind in the limbic area. The programmed mind is sub-conscious, which absorbs material from our intuition and feelings about our world, as received by the rational mind. Below the limbic area rests the literal mind, the mind that governs all bodily function.

Your physical body is composed of many parts which may act in unison or independently. Your brain also is divided into independently functioning units we classify as minds. Your ability to use the whole body or part of it depends upon your ability to use the whole brain and all of its parts.

For instance, you can perform a physical task with your hands while your consciousness is engaged elsewhere and your programmed mind is reacting to stimuli outside of your awareness. Your intuitional mind may be trying to reach you, but you are so busy thinking you pay no attention. All these minds may be active separately and independently of one another.

In their positive, outpouring aspect, all of these minds radiate energy, as well as draw in energy, a function of their negative or receptive side. These energies move or vibrate at different frequencies. The slower the frequency the more solid the mental substance becomes.

The literal mind vibrates at a lower frequency than the sub-conscious programmed mind, which in turn vibrates slower than the rational thinking mind of our consciousness. The intuitional mind is lightning swift, depositing "holistic" ideas into the conscious mind for reason to develop and amplify.

Everyone is equipped with these levels of mind and the frequencies they broadcast, and everyone has "receiving equipment" to pick up ideas, thoughts, feelings and emotions from others. However, not everyone knows how to use their equipment. Just as dogs hear sounds that most humans do not, and bees see colors we've never seen, some humans perceive things that others do not. The amount of awareness of the vibrations around us is directly related to the level to which we have developed our psychic skills.

It is important to realize that psychic skills are already developed to quite a degree on an unconscious level. What we think and feel is being broadcast silently over the airwaves. These thoughts and feelings create effects in our environment which we may not recognize. These mental and emotional radiations are creating the future as they emanate from us. They create conditions which will occur later, and affect current relationships and our own personality. We are unaware of just how much we are affecting our environment. The interaction between the projective unconscious and the reflective unconscious is a continual process creating our world. Development of psychic skills is merely bringing that process into the arena of conscious direction so that we can control the flow both in and out.

Our Projective and Perceptive Skills

The two major psychic skills you will develop I call *projective skills* and *perceptive skills*. A good example of these two in operation is mental telepathy. In telepathy, two people are needed: an agent, or sender, and a receiver. This shows that they are separate skills. You can send messages psychically, or receive them, but not both at the same time. All our psychic skills fall into one or the other classification. You can heal physically, or be healed. You can manifest phenomena, or perceive the manifestation of it.

Projective skills enable you to control the radiating of your own vibrations. When both selves are synchronized into one action, the projection occurs. These skills can be called mind over matter. Among them are: telepathy, psychokenesis, teleportation, materialization and dematerialization, psychic surgery, psychic healing, levitation, and psychic photography. Poltergeists are merely uncontrolled manifestations of these skills in people who are unaware of exercising them. Another term for projective skills is "creative skills," for with every projection we create something. Creative consciousness is the positive side of our psyche.

Perceptive skills enable you to take in information and energy. These are your awareness skills. Among them are ESP, clairvoyance, clairsentience, clairaudience, telepathy, precognition, retrocognition, psychometry, radiesthesia, psychic reading, psychic diagnosis and scrying (crystal-gazing).

The perceptive and projective skills work together but not at the same time. First one operates and then the other. They are analogous to a well-trained comedy team. Neither one steps on the other's lines. Just as the comedy team has perfect timing, so must we when we are working with perceptive and projective skills. They must harmonize with one another, not interfere.

Many people have achieved this harmonious integration of their projective and perceptive skills and have become famous in the psychic field. At one time or another they were all involved with other things, yet with the training of their psychic abilities they left old careers behind.

Richard Alpert, Ph.D., formerly of Harvard's Psychology Department, is now famous as Ram Dass. When he met a revered yogi of India, Neem Karolli Baba, the yogi mentioned that some nights before Alpert had been out looking at the stars, and had begun to think about his mother who had died the previous year. When the yogi went on to specify that Alpert's mother died of a disease of the spleen, Alpert's skepticism of the yogi's abilities disappeared, and he began to cry uncontrollably. Baba became Alpert's guru or teacher, and gave him the name Ram Dass. Ram Dass began developing the same skills and, in turn, is now teaching others.

Other people with trained psychic skills have done many beneficial things. Emanuel Swedenborg, an eighteenth-century scientist and teacher, is an example. Once he was consulted by a widow who was being dunned for an expensive silver service, which she was sure her husband had paid for, but she could not find the receipt. In desperation she turned to Swedenborg and asked him to use his psychic ability to locate it. After three days he visited her to say that the receipt was in a bureau in an upstairs room. If she pulled out the left drawer she would see a board, and if she pulled the board out she would find a secret drawer holding correspondence which included the receipt. The widow declared she knew nothing about such a drawer, but she and her guests went upstairs with Swedenborg. Going through the prescribed operations, they found both the drawer and the receipt within.

Another famous psychic was D.D. Home of nineteenth-century England. His skills were researched by the distinguished physicist, Sir William Crookes, and his feats were well authenticated. Home could make a lever move by merely stretching an arm toward it. He could hold a glass of fluid over his head and in some mysterious way empty it, then have the fluid descend back into the glass and wet the fingers of the person who held his hand over the glass.

Mrs. Eileen Garrett had a long career as an outstanding psychic. She worked with the founder of parapsychology, J.B. Rhine, in the nineteen-thirties. Age was no barrier to her skills. In her seventies, she was contacted by Dr. Lawrence Le Shan, a New York psychologist, who had learned indirectly of a man who had vanished from a midwestern city. Mrs. Garrett was given a square of cloth from one of the man's shirts. Using this cloth, she said he was in La Jolla, California. It was later learned that he had indeed gone there. She also added other details. He was in his middle forties, about 5'10" tall. He had had a loss in his family when he was between thirteen and fifteen years old. Investigations showed that he was forty-two years old, 5'9" tall and that when he was fourteen his father had deserted the family and had not been heard from in twenty-five years.

These people had very different life styles and different abilities. Yet, by training their abilities, they developed skills which made their lives and the lives of the people they touched more productive and meaningful.

3

Getting Ready

It is a lot easier to learn something if your approach is systematic rather than haphazard. This chapter deals with basic skills necessary for a systematic approach. Some of the exercises are to be done alone and are labeled "Solo." Other exercises labeled "Group" should be done with several people if you are to get maximum benefit from them. It is important that you do each exercise in the manner described. These exercises prepare you for what follows, and it is important not to rush. We all have our own psychological rhythm, the way we experience the universe. Adjust the exercises to suit your rhythm, not the other way around. During the course of your study your rhythm will change, so don't be discouraged if you are slow in the beginning.

Focused Attention

The most important skill for psychic development is the ability to focus attention. When we pay full attention to a conversation or an activity, one hundred percent of us is involved. But most of us don't do this. We let things distract us. How often have you thought you were listening to someone speak, only to realize that all the while you were thinking about what you were going to say next, and have no idea what the person said? All of us have been guilty of this at one time or another, so we have to train ourselves to pay attention. Focusing our attention simply requires a desire to do so. Focusing should not be an effort, something we *try* to do. It should be an awareness, something we *want* to do. I have never liked the word "concentration" because it brings to mind images of intense mental effort. Focusing does not take effort. In fact, effort gets in the way.

Exercise 1 Focusing Attention (Solo): Relax in a comfortable position and close your eyes. Silently say "one" and keep repeating it until your mind interrupts you with an unrelated thought. At the interruption, go on to the next number and repeat that until the next interruption. Two, two, two, you will repeat. Then three, three, three. Experience this and be aware of the frequency of interruptions. Now get yourself a timer. Set it for three minutes and do this exercise. When the timer rings, jot down the number you have reached. The first time I tried this I reached seventeen within one minute! Holding your attention to a point is difficult, but the ability to do so will really pay off when you are exercising your psychic abilities, so keep at it. Sometimes it is enlightening to make notes of the ideas and thoughts that interrupt your practice. These often come up because they have not been able to reach your awareness under other conditions.

Exercise 2 Focusing Attention (Solo): Focus your attention on an object in the room. Soon ideas about the object will begin to float through your consciousness: its name or label, its function, its beauty or ugliness, a variety of classifications which reside in your conceptual mind. These are preconceived ideas, rising from your past experiences. Now they are barriers to your present experience. As these ideas come into your awareness just let them float away, keeping your curious attitude about the object fresh in your mind. Don't try to block concepts. Let them flow in and pass away at their own pace. The object is still there when all your ideas about it have exhausted themselves. Now the opportunity for a new view of it can arise. What are you really perceiving beyond what you already know about it? Try this experiment on many objects. Try it on people. Eventually, with practice, you will become skillful in allowing concepts "about" the object to pass away, leaving room for a new experience. Now that all your preconceived ideas of the object have passed away, try to focus on the object again. What new ideas float through your consciousness? The critical part of this exercise is to be able to clear your mind of your preconceived ideas about the object and then to still your mind so that new perceptions, new ways of perceiving the object or person, can come to you from other levels of your being.

Exercise 3 Focusing Attention (Group): Have someone put twelve or more objects on a tray and then cover the whole collection. Remove the cover for thirty seconds and observe what is there. Cover the objects and write down what you remember. Then check to see how many you are able to recall. Also notice how full your descriptions are. This is fun to do with a group. As you practice, you will find that you observe more each time, and that you include more detail. Accuracy is important. Learn to be concise with your descriptions, it will help your observations. Variations on this exercise include walking into an unfamiliar room or store, observing for thirty seconds, then leaving and describing what you saw to a partner. Then go back into the room and check on yourself. How much detail was there in your report? Did you simply note things like the number of windows, doors electrical outlets? What was the floor like? The ceiling?

These exercises will help you suspend your beliefs about things and sharpen your observation skills. We see more when we suspend judgment about what we see and simply observe, much like a TV camera scanning a room.

All things require nonjudgmental observation, before one can really "see" what one is looking at. Early in life, I was indoctrinated to perceive flies around the house as a nuisance, or worse, carriers of germs. They were "bad" and everyone I ever knew was intent on killing them or preventing their presence. I never read any scientific descriptions of flies and their usefulness in nature, so I kept a one-sided view of flies which had been given me by others. After reading the book, *Kinship with all Life* by F. Allen Boone, I decided to experiment. One day in my apartment I spotted one lone tiny fly flitting around my living room. I closed my eyes and willed the fly to come closer, to land on my hand. Presently it did light on the back of my hand. I suspended all previous notions I had held about flies and just experienced *that* fly, walking around on my skin. Do you shudder to think of it? We are so used to shuddering when insects touch us, that it is difficult to overcome the habit, but I was able that day to dismiss it from my mind and really get into those tiny footsteps on my skin. What had always been a disagreeable experience now became a delightful perception of tiny suction cups tracking a delicate line across my hand. Its tiny, fragile quality struck me as a new idea, and I transmitted my new-found feelings of friendliness to the fly. This made me feel good. The fly remained on my hand for quite a while as I marveled at this new experience. Later, lying in bed in the dark, waiting for sleep to come, I heard a loud buzzing from my friend fly as it swooped in the air above my face. My first reaction was annoyance, but I quickly shifted to my new point of view and listened to the sound as if I had never heard it before. It was another delightful experience as I listened without judging, without condemnation, without preconceived opinions.

Can you imagine hearing the buzz of a fly as music to your ears? Well, it was just that to me, and I felt quite sad when the sound stopped. As I drifted off into a pleasant slumber, I pondered the meaning of my experience. What I had done was really very simple. I had simply shifted my point of view. You can do that too, at any time and about anything you want.

Relaxation

If your inner self is to be receptive your body and your conscious mind must be relaxed. Since our culture thrives on tension, it is hard for us to relax. But if you do not learn the art of relaxation, it will be almost impossible to develop your psychic skills. The following exercises are designed to help you rid your body of tension and to aid you in obtaining a state of relaxation.

Exercise 1 Relaxation (Solo or Group): Stand up straight and raise your arms over your head, hands pointing to the ceiling. Tense every muscle as much as you can and then as you lower your arms, relax completely. Note which muscles remain tense. Repeat the exercise until the muscles lose their tension.

Exercise 2 Relaxation (Solo or Group): Be sure you are wearing loose-fitting clothes. Sit in a comfortable chair. Place your feet on the floor and your arms on the arms of the chair. If there are no arms, rest your hands in your lap. Do not cross your arms or legs. This inhibits the flow of energy. Starting at the top of your head and working to the bottom of your feet, instruct each part of your body to relax in turn. For example, "I feel my scalp relax. All tension is disappearing, leaving my scalp free and light. I feel my head relax, all the tension is leaving my forehead, leaving it peaceful and alert. I feel my eyes relax, my eyelids relax, my eyebrows relax. All of the tension is gone. I am energized and refreshed." Continue with the rest of body, directing the tension to sink from the shear weight of gravity. By the time you reach your ankles, what little tension is left can be directed out through the soles of your feet. Do this exercise slowly, with a gentle, almost monotonous tone of voice. The pace itself will relax you.

Breathing

Proper breathing is important to relaxation. Tense people breathe shallowly; those who are relaxed breathe deeply. The oxygen you breathe carries energy to all parts of your body, and carbon dioxide carries waste products away. Tension results from a build-up of waste products. Proper breathing begins with the diaphragm, a muscle beneath the lungs which contracts to push air out and expands to let air in. Learn to use your diaphragm properly and your breathing will aid relaxation.

Exercise 1 Breathing (Solo or Group): Place your hands on the sides of your waist, fingers in front, thumb in back. Get a good grip. You might even push in a little on your waist. Inhale deeply and as you do, try to push your hands away from each other with your diaphragm. The diaphragm curves upward, with the lower ends where your waist is and the top under your lungs. As you expand the ends, the top flattens. This happens because you are expanding the lungs and they push downward. As you exhale, feel your waist go in. It may take a little while to get the hang of it. So do it slowly, and as you do, imagine you are inhaling relaxed energy and exhaling nervous tension.

Exercise 2 Breathing (Solo or Group): Once you have mastered diaphragmatic breathing, add to it the element of sound. When you exhale, moan, with your mouth open. The deeper the sound, the more tension you release. Don't force it. You will notice the sound gets deeper of its own accord. The tension you experience in your muscles is induced by your mind. By using sound, you focus your attention within your body rather than in your mind.

Exercise 3 Breathing (Solo or Group): Place your finger aside of your nose (just like Santa Clause) and, closing off the right nostril, inhale through the left. Close both nostrils, and hold your breath. Then, keeping the left nostril closed, exhale through the right. As you do this exercise, count. Hold your breath four times longer than it took to inhale, and take twice as much time to exhale as to inhale. The slower you can do it, the more effective the exercise will be.

Affirmations

An affirmation is a declarative statement about yourself. The statement "I am psychic," is an affirmation. "I am not psychic" is also an affirmation.

Affirmations are inner-self conditioners. The programmed mind is programmed by affirmations. Everything we say, especially everything we say with conviction and emotional force, it believes. "Boy, am I stupid!" is a negative affirmation. (So, by the way, is "I'll be damned!")

It will take persistent repetition of a positive affirmation to reprogram your inner self if you have habitually repeated a negative affirmation for years. When you start paying attention to what you say and think, you will be amazed at what you have been telling your self about yourself and about the world. Practice being more careful about how you think and what you say. Whenever you notice a negative thought, supplant it with a positive affirmation. Supplant "That was stupid!" with "I am learning from this new experience," for example.

Write your affirmations down. The act of writing the affirmation helps to focus it in your programmed mind. Use the present tense, and state the affirmation of what you desire as a present reality. On the mental level, it *is* a present reality, by persistently focussing on its reality there on the mental level, you arrange for it to become a physical reality too. Use the first person and claim it as a part of your personality and your life.

Remember, the subconscious makes no judgment about what we give it; it accepts everything. Avoid comparisons with other people, times, places and circumstances; these simply imply competition or standards of achievement which are irrelevant. Avoid negatives like "not" or "never." The subconscious language of the programmed mind does not have any negatives. If you put a lot of emotional energy into what you do not want or what you fear, the subconscious can only use that energy to focus on the very experiences you want to avoid. "No" is good for prohibitions and inhibitions. Don't forbid your inner self to do the things you dislike or fear; rather, free your inner self by giving it permission to do the things you like, and it will give you everything you desire.

There is a story told about someone who found Aladdin's lamp. Recognizing it, he rubbed it. Out came the Genie. "Master, give me your command! I am here to do your bidding." The first request was a new coat. As the Genie was turning to go, the person cried "Wait! In Hawaii I won't need a coat—I want to live in Hawaii!" The Genie turned back to take him there. "But I'll miss my friends!" And so it went. To make a long story short, the Genie, called back for a fresh command every time it set out to do its master's bidding, did nothing but spin back and forth.

The Genie is the inner self. Most people have this immensely powerful servant spinning aimlessly, trying desparately to please its master but countermanded at every turn. To avoid this, be consistent in your affirmations. Clean up your habitual, thoughtless affirmations. Make your intentional affirmations clear and consistent by determining what you most want. If any lesser desires interfere with that main desire, then you are well-advised to let them go.

Some examples of useful affirmations are:

1. I am at my desired weight. (Good for dieters)
2. My lungs are pure and clean. (Good for people who are trying to give up smoking)
3. I have what I need and I use it. (Good for exams)
4. I feel continuously alert, vital and useful. (Good for everything)

Say your affirmations with firm conviction and confidence. The emotional energy that you invest in them is as important as the words themselves. What you are doing is reprogramming your subconscious, programmed mind. We will return to this topic in Chapter 7.

Exercise 1 Affirmations (Solo): Make a list of ten positive affirmations about yourself and your ability to train your psychic skills. Then read the list aloud in front of a mirror. Spend time working on your affirmations until the wording is right for you. It is important that the words really express what you want to say so that when you read them out loud, you will do so with real feeling.

Exercise 2 Affirmations (Solo): List three current problems in your life that you would like to change. Write an affirmation for each of these problems, expressed in such a way that the desired condition is already achieved. For example, you feel that you are always misunderstood. The positive affirmation would be, "I express myself clearly and directly and I am understood."

State the problem accurately so that the affirmation will be concise and directed to the solution of the problem. Keep the list by your bedside and read the affirmations before drifting off to sleep, and again in the morning when you awake. Repeat the reading each night and each morning until the desired affirmation takes hold.

Visualizations

The programmed mind responds even more powerfully to nonverbal messages than it does to affirmations. That is why the emotional energy associated with your affirmations is such an important ingredient. It is also why nonverbal messages of others, through their body language, gestures, and tone of voice, have such a pervasive influence on us.

Your affirmations will be even more powerful if you show your subconscious a picture of what you are talking about. You can do this with actual physical pictures. It is much more effective to form the pictures in your mind's eye. This is called visualization.

Visualizations should actually include all the senses, not just sight, to be most effective. Imagine the thing or state that you want. What will it be like to have it? What will you be like? What will it feel like? What sounds will be involved with having the object of your desire? What tastes, smells, etc? Include all your senses in a clear image of what you want, and your subconscious can't go wrong.

Some students feel visualization is very difficult. It is not hard at all. It is your creative imagination that will work for you, whether it is in the forms of pictures, ideas or just "knowing."

When you are trying to visualize, you sometimes find you lack control over the unwanted thoughts and ideas that arise into awareness. They disturb your focussed attention and the image or idea tends to fade or change so you have to keep repeating it over and over again.

The following exercise will help you in developing your visualization skills. Prepare three white cards to use by painting these symbols on them with a soft black felt marking pen.

On the first one, draw a white circle with a white dot at the center against a dark background. To do this, draw a ring around your center white dot, blacken the space all the way out to your white circle, and then fill in the rest of the card outside the white circle. On the second card, draw an equal armed white cross against a black background. On the third card, draw a white equilateral triangle, with the point upwards, against a black background. Draw these in the same way, by filling in the background and leaving the figure white.

If you prefer, you can cut out the symbols from white paper and paste the symbols in place on black cards cut from black posterboard.

These symbols help you to learn visualization, but they also have esoteric signifigance. Their meanings will become clear to you later as you continue to use them.

If you have difficulty with using the cards, draw each symbol in the air with your finger, or draw them in the palm of one hand with the forefinger of the other, while looking at it. This adds a tactile element to the visualization process.

After you have prepared yourself and are ready to begin, select one card, focus your eyes on it for a few moments and then close your eyes and experience what happens. With continued practice, the reverse of the image will be seen by your inner vision, your "mind's eye" within your head. Continue by using the other two cards in the same fashion. Focussing your eyes to fix the image, then closing the eyes to get the after-image within your head.

This can be done quickly, each night, so that you experience your developing ability to visualize every day. It is always interesting to see what is in one's own head, and this practice will develop the power of your own brain to project images into the forefront of your awareness.

Personal Protection

Just as you decide whom to let into your home, so too can you decide what to let into your consciousness. It is important to remember that *you* are in control at all times. Countless times people have said to me, "I have a ghost in my house and I don't know what to do about it." My usual response is, "Have you asked him (or her) who he is and what he is doing there?" "No." "Why not? You certainly would if that person were in a body. Why does the lack of a body make a difference?"

We are all psychic. Our projective and perceptive skills are interacting all the time, though most of us are unaware of the subtle ways in which we influence one another psychically.

Some of these intrusions are not so subtle. The judgments, attributions and opinions of others, sometimes only unconsciously expressed in their body language, have a way of lodging in the subconscious and taking root. The irritation and impatience of the person standing behind you in line can have an impact on you, if there are negative beliefs in your inner self that induce you to assume the blame for other people's bad moods.

Rather than be a target for unwholesome energies, protect yourself. Learn the art of psychic self-defense.

One of the best protections is a questioning mind. A little skepticism is healty. Be a doubting Thomas, require proof, and don't succumb to your own fears.

Affirmations are good protection. One such as "I am open to the best and closed to the undesirable" or "I am protected by the love of God" will work. It is a good idea for each of us to make up our affirmations in our own words so that we are comfortable with them.

Another means of protection is to surround yourself with a positive energy field. To do this, close your eyes and imagine yourself surrounded with brilliant white light. Make sure this "coccoon" of white light extends behind you as well as in front, and all the way down to your feet. The white light has the power to dissolve all negativity. It acts as a shield.

However, if you remember and reaffirm that you are in control at all times, protection should not be an issue.

Now that you are aware of the need for focusing your attention, eliminating preconceived ideas, breathing properly and affirming your own uniqueness and abilities, you should practice these until they no longer require your attention. Before moving on to the other chapters, these things should be second nature to you.

4

Altered States of Consciousness

The development of psychic skills rests on your ability to alter your consciousness at will. You are already operating in altered states of consciousness whether you realize it or not. This chapter will help you identify and understand the states you are already using. It will describe other states you might wish you could use, so that you can develop them.

Consciousness might be described as having all your mental faculties fully active. Anything other than this is a different, or altered, state of consciousness. Among altered states of consciousness are absent-mindedness, daydreaming, night dreaming, hypnotic states, trance and meditation. We spend more of each twenty-four hours in these altered states than we do fully alert.

When you are engaged in a routine task such as driving the car, weeding the garden or doing the dishes, you often let your mind "wander." Where does it go? It doesn't go anywhere, it simply focuses on something other than what you are doing. You shift from drive, or focus gear, to neutral, or daydreaming gear.

Daydreaming is the art of removing yourself from your immediate environment and placing yourself in a different reality. It is not simply an escape from reality; it serves a vital function by helping to keep the outer self and inner self in balance. Daydreaming provides an opportunity to visualize the way you want the future to be. Sometimes you have a mental conversation with someone you are going to see, a rehearsal. You can go over the same dialogue a number of times, changing the outcome so that by the time you have the actual conversation, you will be prepared for whatever the other person says. Of course, it is too time-consuming to do this all the time so you'll probably only rehearse conversations that are likely to be stressful, such as a job interview, a parent-teacher conference, or a personal confrontation.

Sometimes daydreams are wish fulfilling, like a woman imagining a night with Robert Redford, or a man with Bo Derek. When you desire something that is generally regarded as unattainable, daydreaming provides a way to fulfill that desire. Daydreaming compensates for what you lack so that you feel less deprived.

When you daydream about something that is attainable, it is called visualization. The ability to visualize brings you a step closer to getting what you want. You get what you want by focusing attention on your goal and then by directing mental energy toward it. Next, you have to take whatever action is necessary to make the goal a reality. Most people fall short in focusing, not in acting. A clear idea or picture is essential. It follows that people with well-developed imaginations, who are good at creating clear and detailed mental images, have a better chance of achieving their goals than those who do not. By paying more attention to your daydreams and directing them toward your goals, your visualization skills will improve. This helps train your psychic skills.

Absent-mindedness is a negative expression of daydreaming. It occurs when you let your mind slip into "neutral gear," but have no desire to use this gear productively. You are suspended between physical productivity and mental productivity. Absent-mindedness happens when we choose not to pay attention to what is going on around us. We elect to be unfocused at an inappropriate time. This is the lowest energy state.

The opposite of absent-mindedness is "no-mind," taught by Eastern gurus. "No-mind" is a state of alert awareness in which mental activity (such as thinking) is suspended. This condition of unbiased perception is a high energy state. By becoming aware of your daydreams and learning to direct them, you will eventually be able to suspend them and slip into the "no-mind" state.

Just as you have various kinds of daydreams, according to your needs, so too do you have many kinds of night dreams. During the sleep state, your dreams have the same function as daydreams, helping to keep your inner and outer selves in touch and in balance with one another.

Dreaming and the OBE

Dreaming is necessary to all human beings. Studies have shown that people cannot go more than a few days without dreaming, before they start exhibiting signs of mental aberration. The main function of dreaming is to allow your subconscious uninterrupted time to work on the issues of your life that you have been unable to resolve in the waking state. Without this time, severe mental stress develops. Have you ever noticed that you need more sleep when you are going through a difficult time? Sleeping is not an escape from the problem, but rather a time for your subconscious to work out a solution.

Our dreams provide access to our subconscious. Harmonious interaction of our conscious and subconscious selves is necessary to the development of psychic skills, so it is vital to understand and work with your dreams. But first you have to remember your dreams. We are all capable of recalling our dreams, but not all of us do. If you have trouble remembering your dreams, make an affirmation two or three times before you go to sleep, such as "I will remember my dreams." It may take a few weeks to work, but eventually you will wake up several times a night with a dream. Keep a notebook and pen by your bed and record your dreams. In the morning go back over them to fill in details

Once you have trained yourself to remember and write down your dreams, the next challenge is to learn how to interpret them. Some dreams are filtering dreams in which your subconscious goes over all the events of the day. Sometimes these are literal and sometimes they are symbolic. Filtering dreams are usually the ones you have in the early part of your sleeping night.

Some dreams are precognitive, dreams in which you dream something that has not yet happened. This sort is usually clear and easy to recall. Usually the event you dreamed of will happen within the next ninety days. Often, when you experience something that is vaguely familiar, it is because you have already had a dream of the experience.

The bulk of your dreaming is psychological "housekeeping," in which you work on current problems.

There are a number of questions you can ask yourself to help you understand your dreams. Is this dream just a rehash of waking experiences? Does this dream bring me an experience that I consciously fear? If this had been a waking life experience, what would I have learned from it? Does this dream merely reflect what I desire, a wish fulfillment? Is there an extreme in this dream? If yes, am I going to the opposite extreme in waking life? Is this a "tables-are-turned" dream; that is, am I experiencing something in this dream that I put people through in waking life? With a little time and practice, your dreams will help you to understand yourself better.

Some dreams pertain to your physical body. For example, if you dream of bananas, you may have a deficiency of potassium. If the setting in your dream is the kitchen, the dream may relate to diet; if the setting is the bathroom, the issue may be elimination. If you dream of broken windshield wipers, you may have a vision problem.

Because dreams suspend the reality in which we live, some of the events seem improbable, or even bizarre. No matter how weird a dream may be, it has some meaning for your life. If you cannot figure it out, perhaps a friend who is more objective can. If not, let the dream sit in your notebook and go back to it in a few days. Often the passage of time helps to clarify the meaning.

Another thing you can do is to tell your subconscious that you did not get the message and that you want another dream, dealing with the same issue, that you can understand. You can direct your subconscious in the dream state just as you can in the waking state. This is called programming.

There are some steps you can take to facilitate the programming process. One hour before you go to sleep, do what you can to relax your body. Take a warm bath, practice yoga, have a massage, engage in sex—do anything that will see to it that your physical senses are satisfied. Next, review all the events of the day slowly and in sequence as impersonally as possible. The sequence is important. This step alleviates the necessity of the filtering dream. Then determine to what area you want to direct your subconscious attention, while sleeping. Then, lights out. Keep the issue in your head as long as you can without expending too much energy. Other thoughts will intrude. Allow them to float gently aside. Keep your mind on your objective without hanging on too tightly or becoming rigid.

Sometimes mumbling what you want to dream about, just before you drift off to sleep, is a good way to focus your subconscious on the issue.

Programming of dreams gives varied results. Sometimes the solution to your problems will appear the very night you request help, other times it may take a few days and nights. Sometimes you will remember the whole dream and sometimes just the solution.[1]

Once you have mastered the ability to recall what goes on in your mind during sleep, you can work on remembering what happens to your body during the same time. I call this "awareness during sleep." Having once read about this I became determined to try it. One night, as I lay in bed, I repeated over and over, "I am aware as my body goes to sleep. I am maintaining continued awareness of the phenomena of my body going to sleep." This determined concentration only served to keep me awake, so I gave up and afterward drifted into sleep. Suddenly I found myself aware in a totally relaxed, dormant physical body. Exultant, I realized my programming had brought results. I watched my dreams and observed how totally supine my body was. Then I saw how some energy flowed into my legs so they could shift and move. Utterly fascinated, I watched the waking-up process. From a heavy, mattress-denting position, my body swelled with inflowing energy and came to life gradually. I felt discomfort from my position so I began to move and stretch. I seemed to grow larger and lighter as the moments ticked by. I was so absorbed in experiencing my body that I was awake almost before I knew it. The process of waking was a smooth one; there was no sudden shift. Although I have not done it since, it did prove to me that awareness is more a matter of choice than of circumstance.

Some people wake up suddenly, going from unconsciousness to consciousness, as if they had flipped a switch. Others wake up gradually, going through an in-between state. There are labels for these states. The one between waking and sleeping or falling asleep is called *hypnonomic*, and the phase between sleep and waking, *hypnogogic*. As adviser to those students who experienced phenomena they could not understand, I encountered

---

[1]There are many books that deal with this and other aspects of dreaming. The ones I recommend are: *Creative Dreaming* by Patricia Garfield (Ballantine, 1976) and *Dream Power* by Ann Faraday (Berkley Pub., 1973).

quite a few who had a specific experience of paralysis during the hypnogogic transition state upon waking. As they came into full awareness of the surrounding atmosphere, they found themselves unable to speak or move voluntarily. If they became fearful, the sensation was prolonged, but in every case, voluntary movement was restored within a short period. The body, in this case, was slower to arrive at a level of energy required for action than the individual residing in the body. My instructions to those who reported the incident were to just relax, observe and enjoy the experience without fear.

In these in-between states of consciousness, you are sufficiently alert to reason but not so much as to block the subconscious with your intellect. Therefore, you are more open and receptive than usual in these states, providing an excellent opportunity for you to program your inner self. Some people put their program on tape and play it as they are falling asleep so that the message will take root in the subconscious faster than when they are awake.

There is still another level of consciousness related to sleep which, although similar, cannot properly be called dreaming. This area is described as "out-of-the-body experience," or OBE. During an out-of-the-body experience, your physical body is unconscious and your intellect experiences a feeling of being detached from the body, or out of the body. Let me describe the way it has happened to many of my students: "I awoke during the night to find myself on the ceiling of my bedroom, facing downward and viewing my physical body asleep on the bed. I became aware that my body was fully asleep, and I, wide awake. I wanted to go farther down, and stand on the floor, but had difficulty in controlling my movements. I seemed to be floating. After awhile, I did drift down, and slowly came to rest on the floor. As I realized I was out of my body, my mind started to fear that I was dead, and I felt myself being drawn back into the body very quickly. Entering my body so fast caused a physical sensation that was quite unpleasant, and I sat up quickly. Shaken by this unusual experience, but relieved to find I was not dead after all, I went back to sleep." This sort of spontaneous experience can be scary because you feel a lack of control. Once this has happened to you and you find that nothing bad occurs, you lose your fear and the next OBE becomes fun. Remember, you simply have to *think* that you want to be back in your body, and you will be.

I once had a spontaneous experience in which I was unaware of leaving my body, but quite aware of the reentry. Being unaware I was "out" precluded any fear and allowed a fascinated attention to what was happening. I suddenly felt like a disembodied particle on a beach at Martha's Vineyard, one of my old haunts. I found myself about six inches above the sand in a dark night atmosphere. I marveled at my night sight, my ability to see so clearly in the dark. The grains of sand were so beautiful, and so distinct, one from the other. I perceived wholly the sea grass sprouting on the beach in all its stiffness, sharpness, shape and texture. Moving quickly down the beach to the pier, I looked closely at the barnacles. My sight seemed to be funneled through a magnifier, for I saw each one distinctly and could observe which had life forms within and which were hollow and dry. Turning to survey the scene inland, where the summer cottages lined up, I sensed the sleeping people, the quiet of Ocean Park, and I felt wonderfully alive and forceful as I entered the park. As I circled the bandstand, I noticed a small door in the base which I had never consciously noted before, but which my common sense reminded me must have been there, for the band to get in and out of the performance area. In the flick of a moment, I was aware of being seated in my living room at home with my eyes closed. Gradually my surroundings became my reality as I realized I had really been gone. The feeling of reality was no keener now that I was back in my body than the experience I had just had on the Island. It was only then that the realization that I had been out of my body dawned on me. I was thrilled that it had happened to me.

Out-of-the-body experiences are much more common than most people suppose. Many people simply don't remember them. Others assume that they have been dreaming.[2] Initially, OBEs are spontaneous, as are the other altered states of consciousness I have been discussing. Although you can become more aware of these experiences, they happen involuntarily—that is without your conscious direction. It is also possible to induce altered states of consciousness. These happen when we make a deliberate decision to alter our consciousness or give someone else permission to alter it for us.

---

[2]For more on OBEs, I recommend *Journeys Out of the Body* by Robert A. Monroe (Doubleday, 1977).

Trance and Hypnosis

Induced altered states of consciousness are grouped under the general heading, *trance*. A trance is a state in which the conscious mind is not functioning so that the subconscious has freedom to direct you. The conscious mind can provide a barrier to information contained in other areas of consciousness, the information usually obtained subliminally. By including a trance state, the barrier to the subconscious is removed, enabling a fuller and deeper understanding of emotions and actions.

The most widely-known method of inducing a trance is through hypnosis. Hypnosis is a step-by-step procedure through which the subject relaxes sufficiently to let his or her conscious mind cease its activity. The conscious mind moves into a "no-mind" state. One can achieve the trance state by listening to a mellifluous voice repeating phrases that direct the subject to relax and let go of any thoughts. In some cases, the subject is directed to watch a moving object such as a shiny disk so that his or her eyes, or physical focusing apparatus, will tire. The idea is that if you don't focus physically, you won't focus mentally.

Hypnosis is used to find out what is in the subconscious, to put new suggestions in, and to remove old suggestions. Suggestions like "You will not feel pain," are used in situations in which a person requires surgery but is allergic to anesthesia. Other suggestions may be used to stop negative behavior such as nail biting, smoking and overeating. By using hypnosis, the hypnotist is allowed by the client to go straight to the subject's subconscious, which has to be reprogrammed before any behavioral change can occur.

Hypnosis is a powerful tool for exploring the subconscious used by therapists whose clients desire to delve into the causes of experiences they cannot understand. The mind tends to block out what is painful and sometimes all the conscious desire to remember in the world doesn't help. Occasionally the subconscious represses memories so effectively that they are unavailable to us from then on.

If the client is willing, hypnosis can enable the inner self to release repressed material into awareness. This is called "hypno-therapy." If you seek hypno-therapy, I strongly advise you to go to a qualified, trained hypno-therapist. No one can put you into a trance without your permission and willingness, but it is still dangerous to allow an amateur sleuth to even begin to dig into your deeper consciousness, perhaps opening Pandora's box. A clinical hypnotist must be sought if one wants to rid oneself of undesirable habits through suggestion.

One of the most wonderful things you can gain from a professional hypnotist is training in self-hypnosis. How-to books on it offer only a slow, laborious training process, which is not always succesful. Although it costs a lot more, one-to-one training by an expert is efficient and fast.

Self-hypnosis is also called autohypnosis, and some forms of meditation are exactly that. A meditation technique that quiets the mind so you can perceive material from your inner self is a self-induced trance. Self-hypnosis gives you the opportunity to do your own programming, implanting suggestions in your mind, the mind of your inner self. It is a period of deep relaxation, and the body benefits from the rest, too. It can be as refreshing as a good nap[3].

Meditation and Contemplation

There are many ways to meditate, and the student has to discover the right one by trial and error. The right way is the way that is suitable for that person. Many give up too soon, thinking they can't meditate, when the fact is that they haven't found the right method for them.

For years I meditated according to the instructions of first one school of thought and then another. I felt very foolish, and often humiliated. I was "a failure." How I came to that conclusion, I can't be sure, for no one can get inside another's meditation to make comparisons. But my feelings of failure were real enough and I gave up the whole thing. Looking back, I realize that I never had any criteria against which to evaluate my meditation. I stopped trying to learn to meditate and began to search for a clearer understanding of what meditation is. During my search I uncovered many comments, descriptions and theories, which seemed to contradict one another. Finally, I realized that meditation is a label for a state of being in which the active mind has ceased its activity. The active mind just stops "doing" for awhile.

---

[3]For more on this, I recommend *The Relaxation Response* by Dr. Herbert Benson of Harvard University. (See the Bibliography).

Once I had achieved this satisfying definition, I was then confronted with the biggest proglem of all: how to get my mind to stop doing. My mind was so active that it ran along all by itself, and would not submit to my control, my instructions. My mind was so brimful of ideas, worries, thoughts and conversations with myself, that any attempt at relaxation on my part just provided an opportunity for all this mental activity to overflow and run wild. The relaxation exercises were helpful, but they weren't enough.

Then I came across dynamic meditation. Dynamic mediation, or chaotic meditation as it is sometimes called, is a form of meditation taught to students of Bhagwan Shree Rajneesh, of Poona, India.[4] My first experience with this type of meditation came through a recently returned devotee of Rajneesh. The devotee invited the public to join him in chaotic meditation one summer evening, and I took him up on it. Three other people also accepted the invitation. He explained the technique, then played a tape of music with the voice of Rajneesh conducting the meditation. As I heard the outline of what we were going to do, my heart sank. Such antics! Such activity for a lazy sixty-year-old who hated to stir from her armchair, who rode rather than walked! But my curiousity overcame my reluctance, and pride overcame laziness. I refused to admit defeat in the art of learning to meditate. I gamely proceeded to participate along with the others. We all closed our eyes to enter into a private space with no observers, and the music began. The first ten minutes we breathed as fast as we could with our attention focused on the outbreath. That was all. It wasn't easy. I had to stop several times, but doggedly I went on. For the next ten minutes we kept up the fast breathing, but we released our body to move in any fashion it wanted. At first I moved self-consciously, but in time it became natural. The third section was spent in continued fast breathing, energetic movement, but adding sound expression: laughter, moans, and so on. We let the sound out. After letting the sound out for ten minutes, we were to flop on the grass, just flop and "do nothing." I have never been so happy to drop down and just lie there! But this proved to be real meditation. As I lay there I began to be aware of the silence, vast and spacious, filling the

---

[4]Bhagwan Shree Rajneesh's discourses on this and other meditations are found in his handbook entitled *Meditation* (Harper and Row, 1978).

atmosphere. I heard the water flowing nearby, a cricket humming, a hammer pounding in the distance—all delightful sounds contained in this immense silence which I perceived. I felt absolutely peaceful and have never been so keenly aware of being "in" life, being in the world.

Perhaps this meditation worked for me because I have an active mind and an inactive body. By moving my body around, I was able to get my mind to relax. It certainly worked better for me than the more sedentary types I had tried before. This may not work for you, but that shouldn't deter you from meditating. There is bound to be one method that suits you.

The last of the altered states I wish to discuss is contemplation. It is a worthwhile way to hone your control of your own mind and consciousness. Choose a subject or an idea, take it into a meditative state, and hold your attention on it. Let's take the word "sacrifice." I once used that. I took the word "sacrifice" into my quiet, relaxed state, and said it aloud a few times. I let that drop and allowed all ideas and concepts I had held to come in and be reviewed. I finally reached a point when there were no more thoughts. A moment passed, then suddenly an image of a man nailed to a cross came into my awareness. But he was laughing. I immediately gained insight into my misconception of sacrifice. It was clear to me now that sacrifice meant a letting go, a giving up of what brought suffering to me.

However, this was my insight. My insight cannot be yours. Insight and wisdom are not things to be passed on, one must experience them.
I will close this chapter with some specific exercises for altering your state of consciousness, for sharpening your skill in shifting from one state to another and for fine-tuning the subtle organs of perception and action that make this possible.

Giving Your Awareness to Your Body

This exercise will enliven your body as you give its consciousness heightened sensitivity.

Your thoughts and ideas and feelings are energies that permeate the entire physical body. In the following exercise we will direct certain thoughts, ideas and feelings in specific directions through the body. Start up in your head. Be aware of your focal point of consciousness in your head. Imagine this focal point now moving from your head and traveling through your body to contact each part of the body to share your awareness with it. Imagine you are no longer in the head, but moving through the body, stopping briefly at one spot or another and uniting with it, being one with it for a moment.

Feel yourself as a force, not a form, a force that moves fluidly, with you in the center of the motion. Start at the head and move downward, stopping at your jaw, becoming one with your jaw, then move into your shoulders. From there go down one arm and into the hand. Begin to experience the tingle of the parts of the body as you touch on them and unite with them momentarily. With practice, you will recognize this tingling sensation in each part you touch upon.

You can enliven parts of your body with your awareness as a gift of love at any time. As you move your awareness through your body, carry complete, unconditional caring for every part of your body. Begin to experience each part. Some parts are so numb it may take a long time to enliven them and energize them. Learn which parts are so numb they feel dead to you, and give them extra attention. Ask them inwardly what numbed them, what experience they are holding to keep them so stiff and rigid. As they become alive again, stay with the experience, letting impressions of those parts come into your awareness individually. Stay with it as they come alive and begin to tingle and feel once more. You may experience trembling as they do. Follow that movement as the "lost" parts of your body come to life.

Our bodies hold within the muscle structure much unexpressed conflict. Some muscles are under orders to act and to not act at the same time. In the past you may have wanted to do something that your conscience told you not to do, and the poor muscle was left in suspension. You gave it the gas and put on the brakes at the same time! It may have stayed in that frozen position for a long time. You can release it from its prison with this exercise.

Allow the experience of wanting to act but forbidding yourself to act to come into awareness. See it, re-experience it as you stay in tune with the part of your body that is holding on to this conflict.

Let the conflict come into awareness, release those muscles from their tension, and feel them tremble first in tension, then release and relax.

They may appear to swell or enlarge as they fill with lifegiving energy.

Using Sound to Alter Consciousness

Shamans use drumming and chanting to induce trance states. Rhythmic sound, with its deliberate, organized repetition, is transmitted through the ear to the brain. There, it regulates brain waves which in turn induce changes in the body: breathing changes that increase the level of carbon dioxide in the blood, and other more subtle biochemical changes.

This is very similar to the effect of a strobe light at certain frequencies, or any rhythmic visual pattern. For example, the rhythmic flash of a car's headlights on the fence-posts along certain highways have induced trance states in motorists and caused accidents.

I do not recommend using these methods to induce trance because they are too hard to control. We should work to perfect our psychic skills in full awareness, and stay in control of all phenomena that issue from us.

However, music and chanting can be used to alter your consciousness and heighten your awareness at the same time. Music can bring harmony and relaxation to your body and your consciousness. Chanting can slow down a hyperactive mind and induce a rhythmic pace at which your consciousness is receptive and trainable. Even silent chanting, as in the mantras of Transcendental Meditation and in the relaxation response technique, can be used to help you relax, for example, if you are having difficulty sleeping.

I recommend using music to develop your ability to fantasize and imagine. Music stimulates deep levels of consciousness, sending dreams and fantasies to a level of awareness where they can be observed and utilized consciously. I recommend using music that is unfamiliar to you, music which does not bring in personal memories, to stimulate sessions of free fantasy. Mythical, symbolic and allegorical imagery arises spontaneously when personal memories evoked by familiar tunes are not in the way. Some records that I have used are: "Music of Morocco, the Pan-Islamic Tradition" (Lyrichord 7240), "Pandit Pran Nath" (Shandar SR1007), and "The Seven Gates to Consciousness" produced by the Burchette brothers (PO Box 1863, Spring Valley, CA 92077. These brothers have produced a number of other recordings of music scientifically designed to alter the listener's state of consciousness).

To use music for fantasy work, prepare yourself (and others if it is a group activity) with breathing exercises followed by relaxation techniques, and provide for protection (see Chapter 2). Start the music, and relax with your eyes closed. Receive into your awareness whatever your consciousness produces in response to the music.

It is important to affirm that your awareness is increasing each time you do this fantasy work, or you may just drift off into oblivion.

Use this material to know your own self better, to understand human nature better, to enhance your creativity as an artist, writer or creator of an original and productive life.

Music can enhance any exercise. For example, you may decide to explore a particular kingdom of nature. Just bring it into focus in your mind, and then relax into the music and let it happen. You may decide on animals as a topic, or you may want to fantasize about yourself as a member of the mammalian class. Color is a good area for fantasy exploration. You can explore the nature of spirituality, and the spiritual dimensions of your own being as your consciousness depicts it to you in the present experience. Relationships, problems, personality structures, and all sorts of life situations can be fruitful topics for a musical fantasy experience.

The rhythms and harmonies of music are a favorite food of consciousness. Moreover, each of us has certain musical notes and chords that resonate in our deepest being. Finding your own tone or your own chord is a tremendous experience. By experimenting with silent chanting, vocal chanting and listening to various musical compositions, you will learn which are most congenial and easily assimilated and which are repellent to you. Explore your past favorites in sounds, songs and melodies, and see what rises into your awareness from contemplating them.

Use rhythm and music in your daily environment to bring your brain and body into rhythmic harmony. You know instinctively what makes you feel better and what brings disharmony to your being. Let your body respond more than it has been allowed to in the past, and move naturally to the music expressing your enjoyment of its rhythms and harmonies. Let your body express itself as music, as sound, as a rhythmic vibration in its own nature. Be observant as you practice "letting go" to music. Learn to know your own body as it is now.

Notice which parts of your body refuse to "let go and dance" with the music. Ask "Why?" and "How did this come to be?" and keep on asking until responses come to you. Encourage those parts of your body to join in the fun and to become part of a fluidly moving, naturally motion-filled body. If you feel self-conscious or inhibited in this, practice in complete privacy at first.

Dance to music that has power to make your body tingle and want to move with it. The dance movement in Beethoven's seventh symphony is a good piece; another is Pachelbel's Canon in D. Go ahead and let your body lead. Without interfering, observe how your body moves and expresses the contours of the music. Notice which major parts move more than other major parts; then move into more detailed observation of smaller parts. Are your hands expressive and in motion? Is your neck stiff or pliant? Are your feet glued to the floor or do they move around and lift from it with ease? Do your hips sway or are they inclined to stay in one position? Observe what moves and what doesn't; what moves the most and what moves the least.

Music and movement can help you learn about yourself and reorganize your self and your consciousness, getting rid of any blocks to free expression in all areas of your life.

Expanding Awareness of Foreground/Background Control

For this experiment, you need a recording of a group of instruments. Create a situation where you can be alone, breathing properly, relaxed and comfortable with your record player or tape deck in reach.

Turn on the music, and sit back and listen. Just listen as you usually do for a moment. Then select the instrument you want to be in the foreground of your awareness. Focus your attention on that instrument, and you will begin to hear it clearly, with all the other sounds forming the background of your experience.

Shift your attention to another instrument, and experience the change that occurs. The previous choice fades into the background of your consciousness and the new choice comes in, loud and clear to your focussed awareness. Do this with some of the other instruments, and develop your ability to make choices as to what will occupy the foreground of your attention.

You will eventually be able to hear very soft sounds that are ordinarily overwhelmed by the louder sounds covering them and blotted out of our experience. Practice this technique on your car, listening to each part of the motor in turn. First one part, then another. You can become so familiar with the sound of their full functions that you will be able to detect sound changes when a part becomes faulty.

Try this at a party where the babble of voices seems to drown out any particular speech. Focus your attention on one person speaking and that speech will become the center of your experience, with the babble fading into the background. Switch your attention to another person, desiring intensely that what they are saying will come clearly into the foreground of your experience. It can happen, and will, if you practice this technique.

Exercise to Awaken Your Psychic Centers

Sit erect in a straight backed chair in a place where you will not be disturbed.

Using your right hand, place the forefinger directly on the center of your forehead about one inch above the bridge of your nose. Then place your thumb on the right side of your nose near the right eye and your middle finger on the left side, almost as if you were grasping the upper part of your nose between your thumb and third finger.

Maintain this position as you take a deep breath and hold it for the count of ten. As you do, feel the energy running down your right arm, up into your hand and down your index finger into your head. Then exhale. Repeat the exercise five times without moving your hand.

This exercise stimulates the pituitary gland and attunes it with the pineal gland in the center of your head. These glands are the physical terminals of your two major head centers. When they are in harmony with each other, the centers will work together to bring you to a higher sense of awareness. Practice this every day.

It is in altered states of consciousness that we perform psychic skills. The more flexibility you have in changing these states, the easier it will be to perfect whatever psychic skill you desire. The more you can control your consciousness, the more you can control your life. You will be able to say in complete honesty, "I am responsible for what happens to me, and I am capable of creating the circumstances of my life." If one of these circumstances is the development of your psychic skills, then you are well on your way to achieving your goal.

5

How and What We Perceive

In the area of psychic skills there are three ways of knowing or perceiving— clairsentience, clairvoyance and clairaudience. It is important to note that no one method is better than another, they are merely different. Although you may have a natural inclination toward one, you can, with practice, develop the others. It is unimportant how you perceive, only that you perceive.

All three are commonly referred to as ESP. ESP, or extrasensory perception, is the ability to perceive through senses beyond the five physical ones of seeing, hearing, tasting, smelling and touching. Extra, in this context, means beyond, not added on. The five physical senses and ESP are both standard equipment in all humans. The most common of these three modes of psychic perception is clairsentience, a French word meaning "clear sensing." It is the ability to be aware of or know something inwardly, without the use of the five physical senses. For example, you have not talked to your friend for a few days and when you last did everything was fine. All of a sudden, you get the *feeling* that something is wrong. How do you know this? You know this through the faculty of clairsentience ESP.

Clairvoyance, or "second shift," is the ability to see or perceive people, places, things or events not seen with the physical eyes, usually in a different locale from where you are.

For instance, a mother wakes up in the middle of the night and "sees" her son shot in battle, when he is on the other side of the world. Later she learns her "vision" was true. Or, as in the case of Swedenborg cited in Chapter 1, one "sees" an object in a place one has never been.

Clairaudience is the ability to hear psychically. If the mother of the wounded soldier "hears" the sounds of battle, particularly the sound of the gun and the sound of her son's voice crying out for help, then this would have been a clairaudient experience rather than a clairvoyant one. Hearing voices can be especially disconcerting, and a person who hears them needs to learn how to tune them out as well as in.

Mental institutions are full of people who have had the experience of hearing voices, but were not mentally stable enough to be able to deal with the experience. The proper development of the clairaudient faculty allows you to enjoy and profit from the experience without losing your grip on reality.

Although most experiences fall clearly into one of the three categories mentioned above, others are harder to classify because they involve a combination of faculties. Remember that, as you are practicing an exercise to develop one skill, you may also be developing another. The classification of these exercises is an arbitrary one, so don't worry if the result is not what you expect. In all the exercises you are developing your psychic skills.

In psychic development, the first thing you perceive about a person is his or her emotional state. We tend to transmit our emotions without being aware that we are doing so, so we seldom monitor the transmission. We have been trained to think that whatever we feel is ours, and most of us fail to realize how much emotion we project outward. Others pick it up and respond to it. A child is a good example of this. A little boy will reflect the prevailing emotional state of his environment. If his mother is feeling out of sorts, he will be cranky. He doesn't think about it; he just picks up the feeling and acts it out. As we get older, we tend to act out these feelings less, but that doesn't mean we don't experience them.

The problem with identifying emotions as psychic perceptions is that we can almost always find justification for what we feel, so it doesn't occur to us to look for another source. One of the ways to find out how much you are picking up from others is to assume for awhile that nothing you are feeling is yours. Look around your environment to see whose emotion you are reflecting. You will be amazed at the number of times the emotion you are feeling is not yours. Another thing to do is to sit quietly, first thing in the morning, and assess your emotional and physical state. The reason for doing this in the morning is that you are the most centered and clear then, having gotten rid of excess emotional and psychological input during sleep. Once you have a good idea of your emotional state in the morning, then, if there is a radical change during the day, chances are you are picking up someone else's emotional state. As you practice, you will find that it becomes quite easy to distinguish someone else's emotions from your own.

The question arises as to why we pick up emotions in the first place. What good are they? Emotion is the glue in our album of memories. Reflect for a moment on the events in your life that you remember. In each case there is a strong emotional association with the image. Sometimes we remember the emotion without the event. For example, a young woman may have a terrible fear of water without remembering that when she was two she nearly drowned. If what we remember is emotionally charged, then it follows that what we pick up from others is also emotionally charged.

We can pick up the physical state as well as the emotional state of an individual. It is common to experience pain and not know the cause. All of us have heard someone say, "I have a blazing headache and I don't know why." Probably the headache rightfully belongs to someone else. Expectant fathers often pick up morning sickness from their wives. Sympathy pains are psychic perceptions. To know whether or not the pain you feel is yours, you must be intimately connected with the workings of your own body. For example, if your headaches usually begin at the crown and spread to the forehead, a headache that starts in your forehead is probably not yours. We tend to pick up physical conditions from people with whom we have an emotional bond. Whenever you feel something that you think may not belong to you, mentally go through the list of people you know to see if you can identify the person it belongs to. The ability to feel another's pain is a great diagnostic tool, especially if the originator is not very aware of his or her body. Being able to pick up someone's pain does not mean that you have to keep it. Instruct the pain to cease. If it stops, chances are it wasn't yours. If it stays, it's yours and you need to deal with it.

We also perceive intentions psychically. We will say what we think another wants to hear, all the while projecting what we really mean. For example, a guest may tell his hostess that he had a wonderful time, when in fact, he was bored out of his mind. The psychically perceptive hostess will "know" he was bored, even though his behavior did not show it. The ability to pick up intentions is a great asset as it enables a person to perceive the truth of a situation. It can be confusing to hear a person say one thing and to "know" psychically that the opposite is true. Our cultural training leads us to accept the words that people speak when there is more truth in the projected feelings than in the words. When the words and the feelings are different, always trust the feelings.

Children are especially vulnerable to this sort of confusion, because they are so open and receptive psychically. They haven't yet learned the rules of our culture that discount psychic perceptions. When the intentions and emotions of adults contradict the literal meaning of the words they speak, the child must decide which message to believe. The other message must be ignored. Since our culture places so much emphasis on words and verbal communication, it is usually the subliminal message of emotions and intentions which gets blotted out. The child who responds emotionally instead of verbally is considered stupid. But the adult who learned to ignore the messages of emotions and intentions is psychically "stupid!" By developing your psychic skills now you are undoing the damage that was thoughtlessly inflicted on you when you were a child, and you are less likely to pass the psychic handicap on to other children.

Remember, the child within you is your inner *self*.

The first thirty seconds of any experience gives you the most accurate information you will ever have. For that period of time, you are functioning below the level of consciousness and all input is unpreconceived and unmonitored. After thirty seconds, the intellect tends to get in the way, making judgments and comparisons and censoring what it will accept. The first thirty seconds that you know someone gives you the most unbiased and clearest picture you will ever have of what that person really is.

Perceiving intention is helpful even when the words and the feelings do not contradict one another. Some people have trouble expressing themselves clearly in words. They become more and more confusing in their attempt to communicate their ideas. Being able to go beyond the words to the concept makes the whole communication process much easier. People who spend a lot of time together naturally fall into this communication and, to outsiders, appear to speak in shorthand. What really happens is that the communication between the two is telepathic.

Everyone has experienced this kind of connection, for example riding along in a car with someone and not talking, when suddenly she starts humming the tune that was running through your head. Or getting the feeling that a friend or relative is going to call, and then they do, or feeling like calling them but putting it off only to get a call from them.

Once I picked up the phone to call my daughter and the line seemed to be open. I waited for the dial tone. Then I heard a voice say "Hello?" "Hello?" I answered back. You guessed it—it was my daughter. She had just dialed me, but it never rang. I picked up the phone just in the instant that the connection was made. Have you had this sort of thing happen to you?

Factual information is also available through telepathic communication. Where this information comes from has always been a subject of controversy. The great psychologist, Carl Jung, developed the theory of the collective unconscious to account for the fact that the same archetypal symbols crop up again and again in the minds of different individuals and in the art and rituals of different cultures all through history. Esoteric doctrine says that the essence of the universe is mind, in some cosmic sense. Physicists are beginning to agree that the cosmos is much more like a great mind than a great machine. It seems that all thoughts have energy going out into the universe, where it becomes available to anyone who is receptive to the particular quality and "frequency" of the thought. The energy that makes some thoughts "louder" than others is emotion—love, anger, elation, hate, joy, awe, the full spectrum of human emotion.

Danger is the easiest feeling to pick up psychically. People who are aware of no other psychic perception will admit to feelings of danger. This is because self-preservation is the strongest of human needs. It is hard to speak of perceiving danger without using the word "premonition," which is the awareness of an event before it happens. Premonitions are warnings that give you time to make adjustments in order to avert potentially dangerous situations. For instance, if you have a premonition of an automobile accident, you can drive more slowly and more defensively so that the accident will not take place.

One day about five years ago, I was taking a long trip, musing and thinking as I drove along a super-highway, when suddenly there flashed into my awareness an image of a large, white trailer truck. Accompanying that impression was a strong sense of danger. Not where, when or how, just the sense of danger connected with a large white truck.

I looked about me and did not see any such truck, but the sense of danger persisted. Watchful now, I slowed down and drove cautiously. Soon, coming up on my right, the white truck appeared. I let it pass me on my right and watched as it moved into my lane. I slowed even more as the truck continued weaving in and out of the three lanes. My sense that it held danger to me persisted, so I kept my distance from it, but close enough to watch it because I was so curious. Nothing happened. It kept weaving in and out, then it took an exit ramp and left the highway. There was no accident, nothing to prove I was right in my hunch. However, I clearly experienced the sense of danger leave me as the truck left the highway.

On another occasion, my husband and I were driving along a winding, lonely road to our psychic development class around seven o'clock. Suddenly I became afraid. My heart started to pound. I tuned into the fear, and told him what I was experiencing. He did not laugh, but encouraged me to tell him more. Into my awareness came a vision of a car hurling toward us from our right, but far ahead. It occurred to me that our combination of travelling speeds might bring us together at an intersection resulting in a crash, so I asked my husband to slow down. He did, but my sense of danger persisted for a moment, as I saw within my mind the speed and weaving of the other car, appearing to be out of control. Then the sense of danger disappeared as suddenly as it had come to me. The sharp change in my emotional state made a deep impression on me. We never did see another car, so I had no way of confirming my premonition.

These stories illustrate one of the drawbacks in practicing psychic skills: No feedback! Many cases are hard to verify. We all like to see proof that we are "right" because we have been conditioned for a long time that being right is good and being wrong is bad. As a result, we avoid listening to premonitions because they might be wrong, and we set up barriers to the free flow of interaction between the inner and outer selves.

Your psychic perceptions are never "wrong," but they can be used unskillfully.

When you have premonitions of disaster for others, the situation becomes more complex because there is very little anyone can do to change another's behavior. Most people feel that because they are aware of an event, they are therefore in some way responsible. They feel a sense of guilt, when they see something is going to happen. They think they should do something about it. Because this guilt is too difficult to bear, many close down their perceptive faculties altogether. It is important to realize that being aware of something does not make you responsible for it. The ability to sense danger is just part of the design to keep the species alive. If you can sense danger then you can sense other, more pleasant things as well.

One of the ways we sense danger is through our sense of proximity, which is the ability to sense how close or how far away another person is. Most people use this sense when they are asleep, so that if someone walks into their bedroom, they automatically wake up. The introduction of a different energy pattern changes the existing vibratory rate in the room and the subconscious, which never sleeps, warns the rest of the system of potential danger. People develop their own spatial area, known as the critical space. This is the physical area around a person in which he or she feels safe. Anyone entering that space disturbs the safe feelings so that the person is forced to decide whether the intruder is a threat or not. The point to which your critical space extends is the point to which your proximity sense has already been extended. With practice, the proximity sense can be developed well beyond these limits. It can be developed to the point that you are aware of someone's approach long before he or she appears. Spies develop this sense to a remarkable degree because their lives depend on it.

We also perceive the presence of objects, as well as other human beings. There are few among us who have not wished they had developed this sense, after stubbing their toe on something out of place in the middle of the night. Many people blind from birth have a well-developed proximity sense. The reason that this is possible is that everything in the universe vibrates, and it is these vibrations that we pick up. As the vibratory rate changes, so does our perception of a particular space. The denser the material, the lower the vibration. Objects are harder to perceive than living things, since they vibrate at a lower rate due to their density.

We have discussed how we perceive and what we perceive, but not where these perceptions come from. For the most part, we get these perceptions from another person's aura.

The Aura

The word *aura* comes from the Greek and means "breath" or "air." The dictionary defines aura as: "1) Any subtle, invisible emanation or exhalation such as the aura or scent of flowers; 2) A distinctive atmosphere surrounding a person; such as an aura of sanctity; 3) A draft or motion of air caused by electrical repulsion." Simply put, an aura is the energy field which surrounds every living thing.

The aura is a measurable emanation. It gives off both light and heat. The light can be measured through a photographic process, and the heat can be measured through a heat sensing process. If we had access to a motion picture of our aura, we would see that it is constantly in motion. It is organic in that it is part of us. As such, it changes as we change.

If we are happy, it tends to be large and bright. If we are sad or ill, our aura tends to be small and dark. The aura is not consistent in shape or size. There can be bubbles or bulges in various places. Sometimes it will bulge in a round or conical shape above the head, giving the impression of a conehead on "Saturday Night Live." At other times there will be a bulge over the left ear or right eyebrow. Then the bulge will disappear and another will appear elsewhere. These are simply shifting concentrations of energy. The aura is asymmetrical: we cannot assume that what is on one side is matched on the other side.

There are several ways to perceive an aura. One of these ways is visually. If you look at a person or a plant for a while, a white glow seems to become visible, closely adhering to the shape of the living thing. It is easier to see this light against a plain white or light background. The size of this white glow depends in part on the subject and in part on the ability of the observer to get in harmony with the subject.

The size of the aura will depend, in some measure, on the species of living thing. Bacteria are likely to have very small auras since they are very small and simple beings. As living things become more complex biologically, they tend to have more energy. The more energy a being has, the larger and more visible the aura. For instance, the plants in our houses are likely to have smaller auras than the pets. The pets are likely to have smaller auras than the humans.

For skeptics who doubt their eyes, this emanation is easily photographable through a special process called Kirlian photography, named for the Russian scientist who discovered it. The process involves running high frequency electrical fields through living things. By varying the frequencies, different details show up in the photographs. A disturbance in the energy patterns indicates a disturbance in the organism. This suggests that the aura provides an early warning system for disease.

There is a white field of energy close to the body which is easily photographable. The aura property which is beyond this tends to change shape and undulate constantly. It is here that we are likely to see colors. When we talk about "seeing" colors, it is different from looking at a bunch of color swatches from the paint store. We are seeing light, not pigment. Sometimes we will "sense" a color rather than actually see it. This comes from the heat that is emitted with each hue of spectral light.

Light travels in waves. When the white light is broken down into its components, as through a prism, we see the colors of the spectrum. A rainbow is the separation of light into individual frequencies. Each color has its own frequency and together these frequencies constitute brilliant white light.

The colors we see, or sense, are constantly changing, according to our physical, mental and emotional health. When things are going right, our aura tends to be large and bright with clear colors. When we have any sort of imbalance, our aura tends to become less solid, the colors become dull and murky, and sometimes holes appear. The aura of a happy person is almost opaque, reflecting solid energy. An unhappy or ill person has an aura that is amorphous, and in some places it disappears altogether. The energy pattern is ragged with spikes.

Each color has a certain significance. Red, for example, is the color of physical energy. When there is a solid band of red in the aura, the person is likely to be in good physical condition. If red is coming toward the person, he or she probably needs some energy. Clear, bright red is energy at its most physical. This energy can be used to move boulders, participate in athletics, or engage in sex. This energy can be modified by adding other colors, just as you modify colors by mixing them.

White, which is the combination of all colors (remember, we're speaking of light, not pigment), has a high positive vibration. Black, conversely, is the absence of color and has a tendency to absorb negative vibrations. Black tends to lower the vibration of whatever color it is added to.

Using red as our example, if we add white, we get pink, which is the color of love. Red (physical) plus white (spiritual) equals love. If we add black to pink, we get rose, which is the color of loneliness or the absence of love. If we add black to red, we get dark red, which is the color of anger. We have all heard the expression, "He was so angry he saw red." What this means is that this man actually saw his own aura, because the strength of his anger made his aura strong and, therefore, visible.

The other colors also have specific functions. Yellow, the color of sunshine and buttercups, is associated with happiness and joy. It is also the color of intellect, so people who are mentally active tend to have a lot of yellow in their auras.

Orange, which is a combination of red (physical) and yellow (intellectual), represents the assimilation of ideas. It is associated with optimism.

Green is the middle of the color spectrum and it represents balance. When a pendulum stops swinging, it comes to rest in the middle. Green is the color of nature, of leaves and grass. It provides peace and harmony and is soothing to the nervous system.

Blue is on the cool side of the spectrum and as such is more involved with the spiritual than the physical. Blue has to do with raising consciousness, meditation, truth and serenity of the spirit.

Purple is a strong healing color. It is the highest vibration of light and is associated with mysticism. It is excellent for mental equilibrium and has to do with spiritual development and clairvoyance.

When we think or talk about something we are particularly fond of, our auras get larger and more visible. The converse is also true; when we talk about something distasteful, our auras shrink. As you become aware of your aura, you can change the size and shape of it at will. All that is required is mental energy and intent. You focus your consciousness in your head and visualize a change in your aura, for example, a bubble coming out of your head from the left occipital lobe. Have someone who is learning to see auras describe yours. With practice, they will be able to see what you are doing without your telling them what to look for.

When we speak, we tend to send part of our auras outward in the direction of the listener. Sometimes we can see this mental energy coming out of the forehead just above the nose, from the space often referred to as the "third eye." If the speaker is secure and intent, the energy seems to come out in a steady stream, giving the aura a unicorn appearance. If the speaker is angry, the energy seems to come out in spurts, like arrows or daggers.

Another way to perceive auras is by the sense of touch. The aura is an emanation of energy which can be felt. Let me draw an analogy. If you are riding in a car and look out the window, you don't see anything immediately around the car. However, if you stick your hand out the window, you can feel the tremendous pressure of the air around the car. Auras are analogous to this, though much more subtle.

Anyone can feel his or her own aura. You must be in a relaxed state, however, to do this. Place your hands in front of you about two feet apart, elbows bent, hands relaxed, palms facing one another. Slowly start moving them toward one another. You might want to close your eyes for easier concentration. At some point, as you move your hands together, you will feel a slight resistance. At first this resistance is likely to be so subtle that you overlook it. With practice however, you will become sensitive to the resistance. The resistance occurs when the aura of one hand touches the aura of the other. If you look at the distance between the hands and divide it by two, you get an idea of how large your aura is. If you concentrate on sending energy to your hands, you can increase the density of the aura, thereby increasing the resistance.

To feel another person's aura, stand behind that person while he or she is sitting down. Place your hands three to five inches away from the head, palms down. Move your hands around the head, noticing any changes. The aura is strongest around the head and shoulders so it is easiest to feel the aura there. This is not to suggest that you can't feel it elsewhere, because you can. It is just easier where the aura is strongest. You can tell how large the aura is by placing your hands close to the head, without actually touching it, and slowly moving them away from the head until you no longer feel the vibrations. Or start way out and move in, much the same as when you were feeling your own aura.

You will notice that when you are feeling someone's aura, the intensity differs from place to place. Some people will notice a temperature change from one part of the aura to another. This signifies that there is an imbalance somewhere in the body. This is a great diagnostic tool. If a person becomes aware of an imbalance before other warning systems (symptoms) set in, he can obtain preventive medical treatment in the earliest stages. Generally, if the aura is warm, there will be a cool spot right where the imbalance is. If we photographed it, the spot would appear to be amorphous and jagged instead of solid and smooth.

The consumption of chemicals will change the aura. Marijuana tends to make the aura more porous, less solid. It becomes like Swiss cheese, solid in some places with holes in others. The effect usually lasts twenty four to forty hours. Alcohol makes the aura more porous too. It becomes a sponge, and the person loses the ability to shut out undesirable vibrations. Because the alcohol depresses the central nervous system, acting as an anesthetic, the person can't tell how much negativity is being absorbed. Very sensitive people can get a "hangover" from very little alcohol. The hangover is the accumulation of the negative vibrations absorbed when their defenses were down. One drink can change an aura. If you have a willing subject, try a before-and-after experiment. Make sure you write down your impressions of the person's aura before the drink as the changes are subtle and your memory can play tricks.

The aura tells us a great deal about a person even before we have any other input. Remember our previous discussion about the first thirty seconds you meet someone? What you are really doing is "reading" or "sensing" the other person's aura. If you walk into a room and someone you have never met has his or her back to you, without any hesitation you get certain "vibes" about that person. Without even thinking about it, our first response (and we are responding to signals which the person is projecting) is, "I would like to know this person," or, "I don't think I'll bother." If you haven't even seen the person's face and he or she hasn't seen you, the "vibes" you get are based on what is emanating from that person's aura. Experience this at the next party you go to. The point is that we make judgments based on what is in the aura before we get our minds in gear.

If we pay attention to the initial "reading" we make of a person's aura, we can save a lot of wear and tear on our emotions. Experiencing someone's aura is part of the communicative process. We blend it with our logical understanding. In this age of awareness of body language, we assume that we are using our intellect. We are, but that does not negate the fact that we experience the aura.

A way to *really* experience someone's aura is by hugging. When you hug someone, you are totally within his or her aura. In Chapter 5 there are exercises for learning to sense people's auras. Once you become proficient at this skill you will discover that you are able to get more information about a person in a hug than you ever will verbally. Remember, not only do you pick up the other person's vibrations, but he or she also picks up yours. There is a transfer of energy. For this reason, a hug is a great healing device, and a great pick-me-up for when you're down.

In addition to auras, we also get perceptions from places. Just as a trained investigator can tell who has passed through a room, so can a trained psychic. The walls and furniture absorb the vibrations of the people who have been there. An intense emotional interaction in a room will leave a residue even if the people involved have not been there before or since. For example, two people have a vigorous argument in a room and then leave. You walk in sometime after and feel tension and anger. If you are perceptive, you know that what you are feeling is what has been left behind. Otherwise, you feel tense and angry and don't know why. It doesn't have to be immediately after an emotional interchange. The vibrations can stay for long periods of time. The more time people have spent in a particular place, the stronger the vibrations, and the longer they will persist.

Historic places can trigger memories from other times and places. Sometimes we enter a room that feels very familiar, a place that you feel you've been to before. You have a feeling of *deja vu*, a French expression which means "already seen." This feeling of already having been in a certain place or experiencing a certain situation usually occurs because you are tugging at a memory of a past life which occured in that place, or you may be recalling a dream or an OBE (out-of-the-body experience) in which you visited the place. Sometimes you may just respond to the history of a place without any personal connection, and pick up what went on there. The ability to perceive has less to do with where you are than with how you are. Openness enhances your perceptions and closedness inhibits them. The place itself matters relatively little.

Now that you know how and what you can perceive, it is time to move to the exercises to develop your perceptive skills and actually do it. It is important to develop your perceptive skills before your projective skills. Perception is an absorbing faculty by which you acquire knowledge, and knowledge can lead to wisdom. Projection is a directing faculty by which you influence people and things around you; used without wisdom it can generate a lot of trouble in your life. Projective skills should be attempted only when you have achieved a high degree of self-awareness and are in a position to take responsibility for what you send to others.

Keep in mind, however, that some of the classifications I have made of psychic skills are unavoidably arbitrary, and that you may in fact be developing both projective and perceptive skills simultaneously. Above all, they should be fun. Have fun with the exercises; I certainly did.

6

Training Your Perceptive Skills

In the last chapter, I described the ways in which we perceive and what we perceive. Now you are ready to begin to train your psychic skills. In Chapter 1, I divided the psychic skills into two broad categories, perceptive and projective, or receiving and sending. In this chapter, you will work on developing and training your perceptive, or receiving, psychic skills.

Perceptive skills are those skills that enable us to receive impressions, thoughts or communications concerning others from people, places or objects. Perception occurs on a different level from that of intellect, so the first step to becoming a good receiver is to learn to quiet your conscious mind. We discussed quieting the conscious mind in Chapter 2. If you feel you have not yet grasped this concept, review those exercises before beginning the exercises in this chapter.

These exercises are like games and should be fun for you. Don't spend too much time on any exercise. It is better to move quickly from one to another, rather than do the same one over and over. A carefree attitude leads to greater success, so don't "force" the exercises. Approach them with enthusiasm and a "let's see how we do" attitude, rather than "do or die." Forcing psychic skills impedes the flow of sending and receiving.

Never do the exercises when you are tired or dispirited. Boredom kills our psychic sensitivity, so avoid it. Researchers have found that when people become bored with an ESP exercise, they express their feelings of dislike by using their psychic powers to come up with wrong answers. In such cases, people actually get "negative scores," below what they would get by random guessing with no psychic abilities involved.

Telepathic Receiving

Telepathic receiving is something that develops naturally between people who are emotionally connected. You "know" what the other person is thinking or feeling without having been told verbally. With practice, you can develop the ability to receive telepathically from practically anyone.

Exercise 1 Telepathic Receiving (With One Other): Have a friend mentally select a fruit he or she likes. Then have your friend send you a mental image of the piece of fruit selected. Your friend should mentally repeat the name of the fruit several times, and at the same time, visualize the fruit. He or she should mentally describe the fruit to you. For example, after mentally repeating the word "plum" several times, your friend then would visualize the roundness, the deep purple color, the soft smoothness of the skin, while mentally sending you these images. Clear your mind so as to receive what your friend is sending mentally, write down your impressions, then move on to another piece of fruit. Thirty seconds should be sufficient for each one. Then check your answers. Remember that if you do poorly, the fault may lie with the sender just as much as with the receiver. It may also be simply a matter of too little practice. Repeat this exercise with other categories, such as vegetables or flowers. Keep the images simple and familiar. Color is a good category because there are no details to get in the way. If, after a few tries in several categories, you have had no success, try changing your sender.

Exercise 2 Telepathic Receiving (Solo): When the phone rings, guess who is calling before you pick up the receiver. Sometimes you know who it is because you have been expecting the call. You can't count these calls as hits. As you practice this you will find that you get better. The other telephone exercise is to call someone the minute that person comes to mind and ask if he or she has been thinking of you. You will be surprised to learn how often you have been receiving a telepathic communication rather than originating the thought yourself.

Exercise 3 Telepathic Receiving (Group): Gather a group of people in one room—eight to ten is a good number. Ask them to agree on an object to concentrate on while you are out of the room. When they are ready, come back into the room and try to guess what object they have chosen. Most people have little success with this at first. Don't worry about it. The more relaxed you are, the greater the likelihood that you will be successful. Clear your mind of your own thoughts and then try to "tune in" on what the others are projecting. Perhaps you will get a flash of color, or a shape. See if you can connect the mental images you receive with an object in the room. Then make your guess. Everyone in the group should take a turn at going out of the room and then coming back in and trying to receive the others' projections.

Exercise 4 Telepathic Receiving (With One Other): Have a friend collect a dozen or more pictures of clearly defined objects or scenes. Magazines, calendars and postcards are good sources. Without looking at the selection of pictures, ask your partner to chose one. While you sit in one room, have your partner sit in another room looking at the picture and sending the image of it to you telepathically. Write down or sketch any and all impressions you get, no matter how fleeting or incomplete they are. After a minute or so, have your partner go on to another picture. Number the pictures and your responses, to keep track. As you practice, you will find you pick up more details. Compare what you have written and drawn with the target picture. Do you begin to see how some of those fleeting images or incomplete flashes relate to the picture? If, after a few more attempts, you still fail to get impressions, try choosing another person to be the sender.

Exercise 5 Telepathic Receiving (Group): This technique is a variant of Exercise 4. It requires at least two people, but it can be done by a group. Here is how a group would conduct a practice session. Give each person a pencil and paper. Clipboards or magazines in their laps can take the place of tables. Have one person go into another room and be the "sender." All the others are "receivers."

The sender decides on a picture to draw, and then proceeds to draw it. Holding the idea of the picture clearly in mind, the sender should concentrate on it until the leader calls to inform him the others have completed drawing what they feel was being transmitted.

When the sender returns to the room where the receivers have drawn their impressions, the pictures can all be compared for accuracy and the results discussed. This is a great party game, and will enliven any gathering. Try it on your friends some evening when things get dull!

In the book *Mental Radio* by Upton Sinclair, he tells about the many times his wife was able to accurately draw a duplicate of a picture drawn by him in another room. You may find that your emotional rapport with a friend or relative will reinforce your ability to "pick up" their message in drawing form.

Long years of research into mental telepathy indicates that emotional rapport can be an important factor in the accurate transmission of telepathic ideas. Spontaneous cases of telepathy are recorded more frequently between persons of close relationships than between any others. To encourage you in your progress in developing your psychic skills, it will be well to work with a sympathetic, encouraging individual with whom you have a close relationship.

Exercise 6 Telepathic Receiving (Group): This exericse is like Exercise 3, except that instead of concentrating on an object in the room, the participants concentrate on a part of one person's body, such as the nose or left ear or right kneecap. The subject then determines which part of his or her anatomy has been chosen. For example, as a receiver, after clearing your mind to shift into the no-mind state of mental alertness, you may notice a tingling sensation in your earlobe, nose or foot. See if that is the part the others have been concentrating on. It may be a twitch or a "ringing" in a part of the body that is the clue. Or you may actually "hear" in your mind the word "ear," "nose" or "foot" which will be the part the others have been concentrating on. With practice, you will be able to discern how you receive messages directed at your body. For example, you may always "hear" the mental word, or feel a twitch in the anatomical part the others are concentrating on.

Sensing People and Things

Each of us has an energy field which is as unique as our fingerprints. These auras can be sensed by others. With our proximity sense, we can determine where someone is in relation to ourselves and, with more practice, who that person is. Sensing objects is more difficult than sensing people because the vibrational rate is much slower, hence the aura is much smaller.

Exercise 1 Sensing a Person (With One Other): Have your partner remove his or her shoes and move around the room while you are blindfolded and talking. When you say "stop," the person should remain motionless and breath quietly, so that you cannot locate his or her position with your physical senses. Direct your energy around the room, like a radar sweep. Can you "feel" your partner's vibration? It will be faster or "lighter" than any object in the room. Make a guess as to where your partner is in the room. At first you may only get the direction. Later you will be able to pinpoint the exact location. Your partner may leave the room in this exercise. You will discover that the absence of your partner's vibration rate is just as noticeable as its presence.

Exercise 2 Sensing People (Group): This exercise is an extension of Exercise 1. Having developed the ability to pinpoint the location of one person in a room, now work on locating several. Just as in Exercise 1, one person is blindfolded and talking while the rest move quietly around the room. When the person says "stop" everyone remains motionless and quiet. The trick here is to identify exactly who is where. When you first try the group sensing, have each person remain at least five feet from other group members. With practice, you will be able to identify the "feel" of each person's aura. As you get better at aura sensing, allow the members of the group to cluster closer and closer together each time you do the exercise. When you get really good at detecting auras you will find that, even if the group members are standing right next to one another, you will still be able to pinpoint the particular aura of each person.

Exercise 3 Sensing Hidden Objects (Group): Before your group meets, have someone hide two objects in the meeting room. First, have the participants "feel" mentally where the objects are. Then ask them to determine what the objects are. This exercise is a good way to develop the ability to locate missing objects, so the "where" is more important than the "what." We have a tendency to use logic in guessing where things are, so have the person hiding the objects put them in unexpected places. For example, it is more unusual to place a nailfile over a door jam, or a pin on the back of a drapery or piece of furniture, than under cushions or behind a bookcase. Spend no more than two minutes "feeling" where the objects are. You will find that normally your first impression, or hunch, is correct. To be more sure that telepathy is not involved, make sure the person hiding the objects is not involved in your group at all. That way you will be developing your ability to sense objects.

Exercise 4 Sensing Colors (Group): Gather eight or ten swatches of fabric in solid colors. The fabric should be of the same fiber, though not the same color. Natural fibers such as wool or silk are better than synthetics. Blindfold the participants. The object is to guess the color of each swatch. Each color vibrates at a different frequency, so each one feels different. For example, red usually feels warm to the touch and green more cool. Have each blindfolded person hold a swatch for no more than ten seconds and then write down the color he or she thinks it is. After that person has gone through all the swatches, he or she should then remove the blindfold and compare answers with the order in which he or she was handed the swatches. After a few runs at this, color becomes an easy thing to "sense."

Exercise 5 Sensing Playing Cards (Solo or Group): Hold a deck of playing cards face down in your hand. Stare at the back of the top card, close your eyes, clear your mind and accept the first color that comes to you. Turn the card over to see if you are right. Score yourself on a piece of paper. Continue through the deck, checking after each guess. Date your score sheet, and note your mood, the weather and anything else that might affect the result; for example, background noise. Notice whether or not there is a pattern to your answers. For instance, if you consistently guess the card after the one you are looking at, you may need to make an adjustment. After you have practiced with the two colors, move on to the four suits. Then you may want to try distinguishing between the face cards and the numbered cards.

Exercise 6 Sensing Playing Cards (Group): For this exercise you should divide into groups of three, taking turns as receiver, preparer and recorder; if there are not enough people, one person can be both preparer and recorder in the group or groups that have two people.

The preparer shuffles a deck of cards, selects ten and places them face down in an even row, without looking at them.

The receiver relaxes into the no-mind state, preparing to receive impressions, and looks at the ten cards lying on the table. When ready, the receiver places both hands over the first card and, with eyes closed, states the first impression that comes to mind.

The recorder writes down the response, then peeks at the card and records the actual number and suit next to the response, without speaking or giving any sign whether the response was accurate or not. "Pokerface" is the word.

Proceed in this way through all ten cards. The receiver should be observant to inner feelings and random thoughts, mentioning them as they come up so that the recorder can note them too. Seemingly extraneous images and thoughts can turn out to be valid psychic information, unrelated to the card exercise; or they may be reflections of the suit or number of the card even when the "guess" given is wrong.

When the first run of ten cards is finished, discuss the results briefly as a whole group, then change roles and repeat until each person has had a turn being the receiver.

This exercise can be varied as in Exercise 5, just looking for color, then for suits, and so on. Any score over two exact "hits" is above chance. However the results are not really that important—it is the practice that counts.

Exercise 7 Sensing Zener Cards (Solo or Group): This exercise requires an ESP card deck, which you can make yourself on plain, white three by five index cards, or purchase at a game shop. An ESP deck has twenty-five "Zener" cards with five symbols: a star, three parallel wavy lines, a cross or plus sign, a circle and a square. As you did with the regular playing deck, guess the symbol on each one of the cards as you hold the deck in your hand. Deal out several cards face down and guess the sequence of symbols. Notice whether or not you are able to "pick up" one symbol more readily than the others. If so, think about the significance this symbol must have for you. With a partner, you may wish to work with the cards to develop your telepathic receiving skill. Have your partner look at the cards and then direct the thought or image of the card to you. Write down the symbol you have received from your partner and then compare notes at the end. A minimum of ten runs is necessary to get an average of your success rate at this.

Exercise 8 Sensing Coins (Solo or Group): Divide into pairs, taking turns being sender and receiver. Select twelve coins, pennies, dimes, nickels and quarters and divide them into two sets identical to each other. Prepare two sheets of paper, dividing each into twelve. The sender and receiver sit back to back with one sheet of paper and one pile of coins on a small table in front of each.

The sender selects a coin and places it on one of the squares, then focuses his attention on it while the other "receives" the picture. The receiver attempts to duplicate the action of the sender. This is continued until all twelve coins are placed. Then a comparison is made. If more than two coins of like denomination are in the same places on the paper, it shows some receptivity.

Exercise 9 **Sensing a Person by Name (Group):** Select one person as a leader, then, with the group, perform relaxation exercises so that everyone is in a receptive state. Have the leader mention aloud the name of someone he or she knows well, but whom the others in the group do not know. After the leader has said the person's name out loud, the rest of the group should concentrate on this person for a minute or so. After the minute of concentration, each participant writes down any and all impressions he or she has received about the unknown person. It is better to write the impressions down rather than to have everyone take a turn telling theirs out loud, because we tend to be influenced by what others say. Set a time limit for writing down impressions. Two minutes is sufficient; after that your conscious mind gets in the way. Then each participant reads his or her notes aloud. The group leader comments on what is accurate and what is not. Then change leaders and do another round. It is important that the leader know a great deal of personal information about the person named so that he or she can document any perception from the participants. It is equally important for the participants to be unfamiliar with the individual, so that whatever comes to mind is intuitive and not based on previous knowledge.

Exercise 10 **Sensing Emotional States (Group):** Place two chairs in the middle of the room, facing each other, with enough room between the chairs so that two people sitting on those chairs will not touch one another. Choose one member of the group to sit in one of the chairs with a blindfold on. Have everyone else move around and, while this is happening, silently pick someone to sit in the other chair. The receiver, with the blindfold on, should put his or her hands straight out in front with the palms up. The other person should place his or her hands on top of these with palms down. The contact should be minimal, only enough so that the vibrations of the person are perceptible to the receiver. Then the receiver tells whatever he or she "receives" from the other person. The name of the person sitting there is not important; the feelings he or she receives about the person are. The blindfolded receiver should begin commenting on the emotional state of the person he or she is "sensing." For example, does the person "feel" happy, sad or depressed? After the blindfolded person has said what he or she senses about the other person, usually in a minute or so, remove the blindfold and have the person who was being "read" comment on the accuracy of the impressions that the blindfolded person received. Rotate the blindfold so that everyone in the group has a chance at sensing.

Psychometry

Psychometry is the ability to tune in to a person's vibration through an object that belongs to that person. Everything around us absorbs vibrations —clothes, jewelry and furniture, to name a few. The greater the emotional attachment the owner has to the object, and the longer the owner has owned the object, the stronger are the vibrations. Psychometry, that is, reading from an object, is particularly helpful when there is more than one person in the room. By "sensing," or "reading," the object, you are assured that the focus is on the owner of the object and not on impressions from other people in the room. Psychometry allows you to "sense" a person that is not present by merely "reading" an object belonging to the absent person.

Exercise 1 Psychometry (Group): Have each participant, in private, place a piece of jewelry they have worn for quite some time on a tray and cover the whole collection. It is important that these pieces have only one owner so that there will be only one set of vibrations. Like fingerprints, more than one set clouds the issue. Each participant selects from the tray one object, naturally not their own, to work with. If someone recognizes a particular object as belonging to a particular person, he or she should quietly select one of unknown ownership. Do not try to guess to whom the object belongs. Instead, clear your mind, hold the object in your hand, and let your mind wander. Write down whatever flashes across your mind. Do not edit. Notice how you hold the object. If you hold on to it tightly, it may indicate that the owner is tense. Notice whether you hold it quietly or keep moving it around. Notice if it feels hot or cold, or if you get a sense of color with it. A watch is a particularly good object to use because it has moving parts and so picks up vibrations more quickly than something that does not. For those people who do not wear jewelry, a key or pen or wallet will do. Afer holding the object for thirty seconds, begin to write down your impressions. A limit of two minutes writing time per object. At the end of the writing time, have each member stand and show the object picked and then read aloud his or her impressions. After the member is finished, the owner of the object should stand and comment on the accuracy of the "reader's" impressions. This exercise has almost limitless possibilities, because you can keep changing the objects on the tray.

Exercise 2 Psychometry (Group): Select three flat objects such as a theatre ticket, a receipt for something purchased, a letter, a library card, a ski lift ticket, a business card or a snapshot. Put in three regular size envelopes, and mark each envelope with a number or a letter so that you know which envelope contains what. Wrap paper around these objects before inserting them into the envelope so that the contents are not discernible to the naked eye. The object of this exercise is to pick up something about the circumstances of the object or the people connected with it. Pass these envelopes to the participants, instructing them to spend only a minute or so on each. Each person should write down what he or she picks up from each envelope. Tell the participants not to guess what the object is: its identity is irrelevant. After everyone has had a chance with each envelope, read the impressions for number one. After everyone has read his or her impressions, open the envelope and explain the contents. Repeat the procedure with envelopes two and three. This exercise is limited only by your imagination and the number of envelopes.

Exercise 3 Psychometry (Group): This exercise is similar to exercise 2, only for larger objects. One member of the group wraps six objects in separate packages and numbers each one. The packages should be wrapped so that there is no indication of its contents, and set on by a table by the person who wrapped them. No one else should examine them in any way before the exercise. The numbers must be large enough, and the packages placed in such a way, that every member of the group can see them clearly. Each participant takes a paper and pen or pencil and sits, taking time to get comfortable and relax into the no-mind state. When ready, each participant should silently choose one package, write its number on the top of their paper, and focus their attention, keeping it firmly set on perceiving the contents of that particular package. Ask questions inwardly: Is it heavy for its size? Is it metal? Wood? Is its shape simple or complex? Pause after each silent question to allow the answer to arise into awareness. Or, visualize a thin strand of your consciousness moving out like the silken web of a spider, entering the package and attaching itself to its contents as a relay cable, transmitting information back to the mind of the receiver. Jot down on the paper any and all impressions such as shape, material, color, use or any other idea that comes to mind. You may want to draw a picture rather than writing words; each person should do the exercise in whatever way is easiest. The easier it is, the more relaxed the receiver is, allowing the information to flow freely. Tension creates a barrier between the inner and outer selves. The easier the exercise is made, the more swiftly skill develops.

As a variant, each member of the group may contribute one object small enough to fit in a shoebox. The person preparing the objects then has only to place them in shoeboxes with numbers on the outside. This variant presents the added interest of discovering which box has one's own object in it, based on the descriptions. If you are certain which box has your object in it, you should pass over it and work with another box.

As before, there should be a time limit of two minutes. When the time limit is announced, each person should shift his or her attention to another box.

Exercise 4 Psychometry (Group): Billet reading is an exercise in which you can get the answers to questions bothering you. It is easier to start with a question that can be answered with yes or no. Each participant is given identical pieces of paper and pens. Sheets from a memo pad will do. Each person writes a question, such as, "Should I take the new job I have been offered?" He or she folds the paper in half with the question on the inside and makes an identifying mark on the outside. Only the person writing the question should be able to identify his or her paper, so pictures or symbols, such as a star, or the sun, are better than initials. The billets (Pronounced "bill-ay," this a French word for note or letter.) are then placed in a hat or bowl and mixed up. Each participant then selects one, checking the identifying mark to make sure it belongs to someone else. Holding the billet, and without looking at the question, try to tune in to the answer. After giving whatever impression you receive, read the question to see how close you came. An enjoyable variation would be to have your group meet regularly to ask questions that will be answered at the next meeting. For instance, this week ask if so-and-so will call. When the group reconvenes next week, tell the person who gave you an answer whether or not he or she was right. This is a popular exercise. We all have questions that need answers.

Exercise 5 Sensing Pictures (Group or Solo): Have some picture postcards, or pictures attached to three-by-five cards, in sealed envelopes. Each participant must have some paper and a pen or pencil to write down impressions. Go through your group relaxation procedures, then instruct the group as follows:

"You each have a sealed envelope with a picture inside. In a relaxed, no-mind state, close your eyes and open your inner senses to impressions of the picture. What are the colors? What emotions are associated with it? Does it evoke any smells, sounds, tastes, or other sensations? What does it remind you of? Does it seem to have a story? Write down your impressions on your paper. If you have any impulse to doodle or write anything at all, allow yourself to do it. Don't hesitate, do it right away. I'll tell you when five minutes are up and then you can open the envelope."

You should tell the group what you are going to do at the beginning, of course, before doing the relaxation, and ask if they have any questions at that time; this is just a reminder when they are actually about to do the exercise.

You can find pictures in magazines, art pamphlets or paperbacks, art postcards, other postcards, comic books, promotional pamphlets, and other manuals, bulletins and inexpensive books. The pictures should be vivid and striking, with strong emotional impact. Look also for unusual coloring, sharp focus, unusual subject or meaningful symbolism. They should be relatively simple and well-integrated, with five or less focal points (eye-catching features) and a single theme rather than a confusion of several themes. Also consider the tastes and interests of the people in your group.

As you build your collection of pictures, group together sets of those which are most distinct from one another. If the pictures in a set are too similar the receivers may be confused and it will be difficult to determine how well they have done. See that the pictures in each set vary in mood or emotional state, color, subject matter (symbolism, sex and age of people, and so forth), texture, line quality, abstractness, period and background of the artist and so forth.

To do this exercise solo, have a friend put pictures in envelopes for you.

After the five minutes of the exercise are up one person at a time should describe the impressions he or she received and the responses made on paper. Then the picture should be taken from the envelope and placed where all can see for discussion of the results.

The Pendulum

The pendulum is a device for getting messages from your inner self, or subconscious, without the interference of the conscious mind. It can be used alone, to get personal insights, or with another, to get answers to another's questions. In the latter case, your subconscious picks up directly from the other person's subconscious.

A pendulum can be made by suspending a pointed, weighted object on a string. The easiest way is to use a needle. Thread it and pull both ends of the thread so that they are even and about twelve inches long. Next, you need a target. Hold the needle suspended from one hand; your other hand can be the target. Or use a piece of paper upon which you have drawn a circle for your target. The pendulum can only answer a yes or no question, so be sure to phrase your questions with that in mind.

Exercise 1 Pendulum (Solo): Hold your pendulum about an inch or two above the target and "will" it to become still. Say the word "still," either mentally or aloud, and focus your concentration upon stilling the needle. It is the focussing of the mental energy on the idea of stilling the needle that is critical. Once the needle is still, ask a question that is guaranteed to give you a yes answer. For example, if I ask, "Is my name Enid Hoffman?" I must get a yes. Watch to see in which direction the needle moves first. This will be the yes direction. Ask a question to which the answer is no. The needle should move in the opposite direction. Now you have established which direction is yes and which is no. Go through this preliminary exercise each time you work with the pendulum because the yes and no directions can change. Sometimes you will notice that your hand will move. This is because the subconscious mind triggers the brain to send electrical impulses to your hand to move the pendulum.

The pendulum can only help you get in touch with what is in your subconscious. Its accuracy depends on you. For example, asking the pendulum about a future event is really asking your subconscious what it wants to happen. The pendulum cannot predict the future; it can only tell you what you subconsciously want to happen. This is a useful technique for finding out what you really want, especially in emotionally charged situations. For instance, you may consciously think you know how an event is going to turn out, but the pendulum, when asked, indicates the opposite of what you thought. This discrepancy points out an area of conflict within your personality and you should consider the implications of holding two opposing viewpoints.

Exercise 2 Pendulum (Solo): Make a list of twenty yes/no questions about current events in your life. Write your conscious answers down, next to the questions. Then use the pendulum on the questions. Do the answers agree? If not, try to figure out why. Keep the list. As the events unfold, check the actual outcome with your conscious answers and with the pendulum answers. Who has more hits, you or the pendulum?

Exercise 3 Pendulum (Solo): The other area of information that the pendulum can help you get at is the subliminal psychic impressions your subconscious picks up from other people. Select a situation in which you vaguely felt you were not being told the straight story. Make a list of yes/no questions concerning the situation; that is, was person X telling me the whole story about situation Y? Was person X consciously lying? Keep a record of questions and pendulum answers; try to find out the "behind-the-scenes" information, and compare the truth with responses you got from the pendulum.

The pendulum can be an absorbing and fascinating tool, but remember it is only that: a tool for focusing different levels of awareness. Eventually, as your subconscious and conscious mind work together, you will be able to dispense with the pendulum and get a psychically based answer when you ask a mental question.

Automatic Writing

Like the pendulum, automatic writing is an "automatism," a way of getting information from your inner self without the interference of the conscious mind. With all automatisms there are basic precautions and ground rules to be observed.

In popular belief, these tools are controlled by outside entities and forces. Never subscribe to that belief. It is unhealthy. It actually constitutes an instruction to your inner self to give up control of your nervous system.

Other beings, both in the body and discarnate, can and do take over the nervous systems of people who open themselves to being controlled in this way. Even where this is a successful partnership, resulting in otherwise untalented people transcribing music by great composers or paintings by great artists, it almost always results also in tremendous difficulty and confusion in the life of the "host." You are here to live your own life. You got yourself born and went through the trouble of growing up and learning to be adult for your own purposes. To give this up in favor of some other being's purposes is a form of suicide.

The great artists and writers are the exception. Usually the parasitic beings who take over when a person has given up control are of a pretty low quality, and not very considerate of your welfare. Higher beings would never be so impolite as to invade your personal, private space. Furthermore, you are not being considerate of their welfare by inviting them to do this. Remember, free will is a law of nature. If they violate it they suffer the consequences of confusion and delay in their own growth process.

Automatisms like automatic writing should be used only for opening up better communication with your own inner self. It is your inner self which controls your nervous system, and thereby controls the "automatic" tool you are using. With training, your inner self can transmit vast amounts of information to you. It can contact the minds of other people, even those who have died or who are not currently in a body, and relay what they might like to communicate to you, speaking for them. It will use its own vocabulary for the most part, since the communications themselves will come in the form of impressions or ideas to be transcribed into words by your inner self.

With all automatisms, never continue beyond reasonable time limits. Never allow yourself to get carried away with the practice so that you get tired and lose control. Never give your own consciousness the idea that it is the boss. Mental institutions are full of people who have given control of their lives to their subconscious minds. Always guide your inner self as its leader, setting down clear guidelines and limitations for each session.

Automatic writing is usually done with a pen or pencil, but if you are a skilled typist you can use the typewriter. Sitting in front of the typewriter, or with a pad and pencil, let your mind go blank. Relax into the no-mind state and wait there, expectantly. In a short while your hands will "automatically" begin to write or type. Do not read what your hands have written until they have stopped.

To "prime the pump," give your inner self a subject to write about, or ask it questions that it can answer. Send energy to the writing hand to be expended on the paper.

If the typewriter or pencil is difficult for you, because of a reluctance of your conscious mind to let go of your hands in the no-mind state, a planchette may help.

Planchette is a French word meaning "little board," and that is just what it is. It is made from a piece of light plywood with three short pieces of dowel for legs. The plywood should be cut and sanded in a triangular shape; one side of the triangle should be broad enough for your four fingertips to rest on it lightly, and the other two sides should come to a point that rests just under the heel of your palm. Round off the corners and edges and put the legs, half to three-quarters of an inch long, under each corner. Finally, a hole must be drilled just large enough to hold a soft-lead pencil firmly in an upright position with the point resting on the paper beneath.

To use the planchette, prepare yourself as described above for automatic writing in general. Close your eyes and visualize the action of the planchette moving across the paper, writing legibly under the power of your own autonomic nervous system.

The planchette is like training wheels on a bicycle: you may need or want it at first, but you will soon outgrow it. Also like learning to ride a bicycle, patience is necessary until your subconscious mind catches on. If you are not successful at first, don't give up. Say an affirmation every day claiming the ability to write automatically. Set up a quiet time, at the *same* time each day, and do not let anything interfere with this appointment. Fifteen minutes a day is a good start. Do not be anxious; worry blocks the flow.

Exercise 1 Automatic Writing (Solo): Set aside fifteen minutes and sit in front of a typewriter, or place a pad in front of you and loosely hold a pen in your hand. Clear your mind; then make a statement such as, "I would like some information about X . . ." (whatever area of your life you feel needs attention). Then sit quietly and wait. When you maintain the no-mind state for a few minutes, you will be surprised to see your hands start writing or typing in response to your request. The request for information helps to focus the subconscious. Try not to read what you are writing until your hands stop. Then read what you have written and see how it relates to your original request.

Some people are naturally adept at automatic writing and have spectacular success with it the first time. Others may find it takes a much longer time to develop this skill, usually due to a mental block in allowing the hands to operate independently of the self.

Automatic Art

Automatic art is just like automatic writing, except that the unconscious mind produces nonverbal artistic expressions instead of writing. It is less commonly attempted than automatic writing.

For materials, you will need whatever artists' supplies are necessary for the type of art you intend to produce: pencils, charcoal, pen and ink, water colors, oils, brushes, paper or board, whatever tools and media are required.

Set up your materials on a table at which you will sit. Your board or paper should lie flat on the table with your tools and colors near at hand. Pick up your brush (or whatever) and lightly poise it over the paper. Wait for the arm to move in whatever direction it wants to, toward whatever supply it might want to use. Allow free arm motion, and wait patiently for your inner self to respond to your request.

To begin with, your target should be pretty specific, a request for a picture of an animal or a flower, for example, so that your inner self has only to work out the details. You may want to keep your eyes open to be sure the work is being done on the paper and not on the table, in case the paper should move around. As soon as one sheet is done, remove it with your free hand to expose a fresh page. Make it easy and comfortable for your inner self to express itself in response to your wish.

As with automatic writing, suspend judgment until you are done.

The Ouija Board

Most people have at least heard of the ouija board. This is a patented "game" that uses a planchette to spell out words and give information beyond the normal means. You can buy one or make your own.

An upside-down wineglass works very well as a planchette. Other types of glass are all right but tend to be too heavy. The board must be smooth and free from bumps and obstructions, a piece of fiberboard or polished wood, or perhaps a piece of oilcloth stretched tightly over a surface. Place the letters of the alphabet, the numbers one through nine, and one "yes" and one "no" in a circle around the perimeter of the board. Either glue them in place or lay them out each time, stacking them like playing cards for storage. Keep it simple.

When your board is ready, your glass is placed upside down in the center of the board. Two people sit opposite one another with their fingertips resting lightly on top of the planchette. A question is posed, and soon the planchette moves to a series of letters and numbers.

The planchette is moved by the nervous systems of the two people touching it. Usually the strongest inner self takes over control and the other just goes along for the ride, to furnish energy. In that case, clearly spelled out answers may be quickly produced. However, if the two people compete for control, you will get seeming nonsense as they shift back and forth.

Foolish questions get foolish answers; incorrect questions get incorrect answers; improper questions get improper answers; impossible questions get answers with no real meaning. In the beginning, most of the responses are usually garble. If there is a need to communicate something, your inner selves will find a way, with or without a planchette. If there is no need to communicate something specific, it is just an amusing game. Your inner selves can make up wonderful stories for you, amusing you and entertaining you by fulfilling your expectations and conning you into thinking the stories are true.

Table Tipping

Table tipping is more dramatic than the other automatisms described here, simply because of the amount of energy involved. It is clear that no one could be consciously "fudging" to make it work.

Gather four or more friends around a solid table of any size, as long as it is large enough for each person to have a place to sit around the edge. Each participant goes into a relaxed no-mind state with fingertips resting lightly near the edge of the top of the table, waiting patiently but expectantly for the energy to move through the hands into the wooden table to create the context within which it can move.

Begin each session with a powerful and sincerely meant exercise for protection, for this sort of event exerts a powerful attraction. Agree on your specific purpose for the session ahead of time. Often people use this method to communicate with discarnate beings, such as those whose physical bodies have died. Specify what kind of being you want to communicate with or you may get undesirable characters dropping in and causing difficulties. If you urgently need some information from some specific person, request that person to communicate with you and answer your questions. A real human need invokes psychic phenomena more strongly than anything else.

Communication is pretty much limited to yes-or-no questions. Be sure of your code before you start, for example one tap meaning "yes" and two meaning "no."

You may just want to spend a short session using your combined energies to make a table jump up and down. It is certainly an interesting phenomenon. In this respect, it comes under psychokinesis in the next chapter. This is an example of how any division of psychic skills into categories must be arbitrary, with a lot of overlap.

Dowsing

Dowsing is the use of an instrument in your hands as an extension of your nervous system to give you information about subtle energy fields around you. Everything has its unique aura. Inanimate objects of the same substance generally differ only as to purity, quantity and movement. Since our bodies contain within them every substance on Earth, our inner selves are thoroughly familiar with them. The inner self also knows what is lacking and what is in excess in the body.

Real need is always an important ingredient in psychic phenomena. When successful dowsers were tested in Britain they failed. This was because there was no real need, only scientific curiosity and skepticism. When there was a real need to be met, their inner selves came through as usual.

Treat your inner self with respect. Remember, if you act as if your inner self deserves no respect, it will believe you and will respond accordingly. Never exercise any psychic skill in a silly, frivolous way.

Dowsing has a very long history. Some people believe that the

Egyptian Ankh or "cross of life" held by the Pharoahs was a dowsing instrument. "Water witching" is known all over the world, usually done with a green Y-shaped branch cut from a hazel tree in European cultures. Farmers and householders have used this method for ages to find water for their families and their animals. In China, dowsing is used to determine proper sites for factories, schools and other specific uses, as it has been continuously since ancient times.

Nearly every country today has its association of dowsers. I am a member of the American Society of Dowsers, Inc. (in Danville, Vermont 05828). They hold an annual convention in Danville every September. I have attended six of these. They welcome beginners, so if you are at all interested arrange to go and attend the beginners' classes. You can hear fascinating stories from the oldtimers, and reports of scientific research on dowsing. Write to them for information about dowsing.

My favorite dowsing tool is the pendulum. I use it for many purposes. Through the pendulum, my inner self tells me my body's needs for vitamins and minerals, its physical condition and other needs. It tells me how it feels about my plans and projects. This is something I need to know because without its help and cooperation I can accomplish little. It tells me about other people's moods and feelings, their physical health, and much more.

I have described the use of the pendulum in some detail in my book *Huna* (Para Research, 1976). There are several other good books on the use of the pendulum for unusual purposes. Christopher Hills has written *Nuclear Evolution* and *Supersensonics* (University of the Trees Press). William Finch's *The Pendulum and Possession* Esoteric Publications, Inc., P.O. Box 11288, Phoenix, AZ 85017 (1971) and Max Freedom Long's *Psychometric Analysis*, Devorss & Co. (1959) are both good.

Dowsing can also be done with other tools. The three most commonly used are the "Y-Rod," "L-Rod" and "Bobber."

The "Y-Rod" is the familiar forked stick, also called a "witching stick" or "witch's wand." Many dowsers claim fruit trees make the best, others vote for willow or hazel. Whatever the source, it should be green, live wood freshly cut for each dowsing job.

Because cutting a new rod each time is a bit of work, many dowsers prefer fastening two lengths of plastic at one end, then spreading the two free ends in their hands to form a fork. Others get such a strong reaction that ordinary tools break or fail to work, so they use a steel rod bent into a "U" shape.

Whatever the shape or material, the two ends of a "Y-Rod" are held in the two hands with the palms up, thumbs out; the apex of the "Y" is pointed forward. When the dowser passes over some of the substance he or she has requested the subconscious to locate, the point of the rod is pulled down.

"L-Rods" can be made from two lengths of coat-hanger wire. Just cut off the hooks of two coat-hangers, straighten the wire, and make a right-angle bend about four inches from one end.

To minimize discomfort due to their rubbing against your skin, you can place these "handles" in copper tubing, plastic tubing, or even a bottle, so that they can swing freely.

Hold the rods so that they both point forward, parallel to each other and to the ground. When you pass over your target they will move; it doesn't matter whether they move together, pointing toward each other, or apart. When they are perpendicular to your direction of walking, you are directly over your target.

A bobber is made from a two or three-foot length of stiff wire with an object like a ball stuck on the end. Hold it horizontally in front of you and walk slowly, keeping the bobber steady. When you near your target, the bobber will be drawn down toward it.

You can train your inner self to communicate through these dowsing tools by setting a known target, like a glass of water, on the floor. As you walk over it, consciously make a minor adjustment of hand tension that will move the rods. Talk to your inner self and tell it that is what you want it to do. This may not be necessary, however. If you get an indication of water other than over the glass, you might check the basement to see where the water pipes are. Below that, there might be underground streams. You may not need any training to pick these things up.

You can even use a map for dowsing! Hold a pencil in one hand and your pendulum (or a small L-Rod) in the other. Ask your self to move the pendulum clockwise as long as you are moving toward the target, and counterclockwise whenever you are moving further away. Start with your pencil at the top left of the page and move toward the right. When the pendulum slows down to reverse its swing, slow down your motion with the pencil and mark an "X." Continue "scanning" across the page from left to right, dropping lower with each scan and making a mark each time where the direction changes. Then repeat the process scanning from top to bottom, with your first pass in the left margin and your last pass in the right margin. When you are finished, examing the pattern of X's to see the location of your target.

Dowsing can be used to find lost people or lost objects. It can be used to locate hidden pipes or electrical wiring, for example, around your home. Many dowsers first dowse a map or house plan, and then go out to the actual location to verify their findings and pin the target down more closely. The map can just be a sketch. Henry Gross, the famous Maine dowser, has located oil and water in Texas without leaving his Maine home.

Psychic Perception in the Occult Arts

The occult arts include palmistry, Tarot card reading, astrology, scrying, *I Ching* divination and tea leaf reading. All these arts are based on objective practice which serve as a vehicle for subjective, psychic processes.

As with all the other practices described in this book, the first prerequisite is to relax, to slow down the thinking, reasoning left hemisphere of the brain, to quiet your emotional states, so that the intuitive right hemisphere of the brain can allow you to tune in to your psychic perceptions.

For example, in palmistry you should first hold or view the client's hands in a relaxed, quiet state, without thinking about them or planning what you will do. This allows you to tune in to the person's needs so that your reading is tailored to fit them. What is important to the client then comes to the fore in your reading.

Or with a Tarot reading, a preliminary period quietly gazing at the spread of cards without personally motivated thought or feeling will allow the prominant features and themes of the reading to attract your eyes.

I will discuss here two of these arts in some detail, the *I Ching* and scrying (crystal ball reading).

The I Ching

The *I Ching* (pronounced "ye jing" in Chinese, but "ee ching" by most Americans) is a very ancient book of esoteric Taoist and Confucian wisdom from China. It means "Book of Change," and it deals with the changing patterns of influences in any life situation, offering advice on the most appropriate way to proceed.

I prefer the translation published by Princeton University Press in their Bollingen Series. This was translated into German by the great scholar Richard Wilhelm, and then into English from German by Carey F. Baynes. There are other translations, such as that by John Blofeld, and another by R.G. Siu, that are useful for added insight or clarity here and there.

Every situation, according to the Taoist wisdom of the *I Ching*, is comprised of various patterns of two basic qualities or energies, yang and yin. Yang is basically creative, positive and assertive, and yin is basically negative and receptive. In the symbolism of the *I Ching*, yang is represented by a solid horizontal line, and yin is represented by a broken horizontal line.

The basic symbols of the *I Ching* are groups of six lines, called *Kua* (pronounced "gwa" in Chinese, usually translated "hexagram" in English). There are sixty-four of these. There is a traditional image and interpretation associated with each one. The text describes how this can be applied to various situations, with six stages of its development and the variations that can occur at each step. It depicts the many choices we have at each stage in the cycle of development of any situation, and always indicates what the wise choice would be.

To use the *I Ching* as an oracle you can use coins or yarrow stalks. Yarrow grows commonly all over the world as a weed, so the Chinese felt that it was in touch with the currents of change prevalent in the world. It is the same with coins. They should be coins that circulate most freely in the world, such as pennies. To get fancy Chinese coins with a hole in the middle is not necessary.

In numerology all over the world odd numbers are yang or masculine because they cannot be divided in two, and even numbers are yin or feminine because they can be. To cast the oracle with coins, you assign the value three to "heads" and two to "tails." Shake up three pennies in your hands and drop them on the table or floor. Total up the value of the three coins. This is the value of the bottom line of the hexagram. If it is an even number, it is a broken line; if it is an odd number it is a solid line. Six and nine indicate changing lines, in process of changing from one value to the other. For six, place a small "x" in the open space in the broken line; for nine, place a small "o" in the center of the solid line. Toss the coins six times until you have the whole hexagram.

Then turn to the back of the book (in Wilhelm/Baynes translation) for the chart which shows you where to find each hexagram. Find the bottom trigram (three lines) in the left margin of the chart, and the top trigram across the top of the chart. Where the column and row intersect is the number of the hexagram you have thrown.

When you turn to the text for your hexagram, take a moment to deepen the relaxed, contemplative state induced by manipulating the coins (or yarrow stalks, if you learn the longer, more ritualistic method). Read through the text without being in a hurry to draw conclusions from it. If there are any changing lines, read the special text that pertains to them. These are areas where the development of the situation is most in flux, and therefore most subject to your influence.

Sit with the images and ideas you have just read for a while, mulling them over as you might review a dream when you first awaken in the morning. Then write down the result of your oracle as clearly as you can.

To understand the *I Ching*, you must first phrase your questions very clearly. One way, useful for all psychic tools, is to make a wish: what do you want to happen? Then ask for the truth about that. What you want from the oracle is the truth about the thing you desire to happen.

Sometimes you have to really think about the answers; at other times it may be so obvious that you have to laugh with the recognition. In either case, the *I Ching* is a genuine well of great wisdom, describing the principles of wise conduct as they vary in practice from one situation to another.

Ultimately, the answers are not in the book, but within you. The book only serves to trigger the wisdom that is already within you, and bring it into awareness. All the answers you will ever need are deep within your own consciousness. The *I Ching* is one effective way to bring these answers to the surface for you.

Scrying

Can you conjure up in your mind an image of a turbanned figure bending over a large crystal ball in a dimly lit room? That's scrying. That person is able to project images from his or her own consciousness out and into that crystal ball so that they can then be seen objectively with physical eyes. Most people just have no idea where these pictures come from, and most believe they are created by agencies other than their own consciousness.

A friend of mine, a young girl, has the eerie experience every now and then of seeing visions in large plate glass windows of stores as she approaches them from certain angles. These spontaneous and unasked for experiences are startling, but exactly like gazing into a crystal ball.

Scrying can be done with various objects, such as a crystal ball (now usually made of plastic), a large, glossy black enameled piece of metal, or even a bowl of clear water with no designs on the bottom. These must be placed on black velvet to induce the phenomenon.

You can make your own device, or purchase one. Before you make or purchase a scrying device, consider the fact that this is one psychic skill that takes many hours of practice before getting any results. If you are easily discouraged, scrying is not for you. Read through the following description of the way it develops to see if you have the patience to accept each small step along the way, and the determination to continue until you are able to actually see an image in your scrying device.

Proceed as usual through breathing and relaxation techniques until you are quite comfortable and relaxed. Then focus your eyes on the device with the mental idea that you can see into its depths. Focus your attention into the depths, bypassing the surfaces. This takes skill! Finally the surface will disappear for you and you will experience viewing it in depth. Keep on practicing this daily, and be patient for the next experience: clouds of mist seem to form in front of you, moving and shifting. They seem to fill this interior you are now able to see. After many practice sessions, the initial mist disappears and the interior takes on greater depth and becomes intensely dark. Each session will follow this sequence: you will see the surface, then the interior, then the mists form and flow, and finally they disappear and give way to intense depth and darkness. Now your instrument and your skill are ready to use for visions. Many sessions may have to follow these sequences and end there before a vision appears, but for the patient, determined scryer, it is bound to happen at some point. From there on it's "olly, olly, in-free" for your apprentice days are over and now you can call yourself a Scryer with a capital S.

A help in firming up your determination to become a scryer will be the knowledge that it is a skill that will enable you to help many people, by seeing for them what is invisible to their senses. It can bring you self-understanding and can be a meaningful and worthwhile activity.

This is an ancient skill, with few people interested today in taking it up because of the arduous training period. So you could be a big frog in a little puddle, if that's your preference.

For a black scrying device of your own making, get a piece of metal, square or oblong and paint it with a high gloss black paint. Make sure there are no ripples, flaws or spots in the finished surface.

Keep your device away from the touch of others, so that it will only absorb radiation from you and become an extension of yourself. Keep it wrapped in black velvet to keep out all radiation of color other than your own auric emanation. Always put your piece of black velvet underneath your scrying device when you practice, whether it is a crystal bowl filled with water, a glossy black surface or a crystal (or plastic) ball. Keep it put away in a closed, dark place when not in use.

Once you are able to see images, bring your other senses into play to understand what the images mean. They could be literal pictures or symbolic images, and sometimes you have to pose the question, "Which?" Usually if the image is very far away, it implies far away in time, past or future. If it seems near you, it is near in time, past or future. Silently ask which, and the answer should rise into your awareness. Ask your inner self about anything that puzzles you, and let it help you interpret what is being seen. What does it mean if it moves in from the left? The right? Ask your self.

After you are skilled in gaining spontaneous projections in your scryer, you can begin making definite requests for specific targets.

Precognition

You can do this solo, or with another, which is much more fun. Each should start a new notebook for this specific practice, and record everything imagined during the practice session, with appropriate notes of date, time, weather and mood.

Begin each session with your favorite method of relaxation. Get very comfortable as you stay aware that this is *not* forecasting, but practicing with your imagination to allow images and ideas to form in your mind without effort or tension.

Begin counting yourself down into a more relaxed state of awareness. Count from ten down to one. Pretend you are on an escalator, riding easily into the depth of your own consciousness. After the first count-down, ask your inner self to present to you a past event of an impersonal nature, something on a newsworthy scale that you have experienced in the past. Wait until something appears. Note and observe carefully what it is, when it was, and your own reactions to this memory.

Now do another countdown. This time tell yourself you are moving ahead instead of back, and while counting, imagine you are poised on a leaf that is floating into the future. If you prefer, imagine yourself on a magic carpet, but it is important that you clearly state you want to move into a future time, into a time when events have not yet become objective. At the count of one, silently state that you are in the future now, and ask your self to present to you an image or idea of some event. Wait patiently, without trying, for something to arise into your mind.

When you have noted and observed everything that comes into your mind, open your eyes and begin recording the whole experience, both the past memory and the imagined future event. This is just a training session for the part of you that has a latent ability to tune into future events. Through frequent practice sessions you will develop that ability. Leave room in your notebook to make comments about this experience later. Listen to the news daily, and note down any similarities to what you perceived. If you watch the news on TV, you can utilize that as a medium of communication to your inner self. When you practice pre-cognition, imagine perceiving a television newscaster announcing an important event, then watch the television coverage of the event on your inner screen.

One-To-One "Readings"

Having developed your receptivity through the exercises given above, you may want to explore your ability to do readings without any tools or props whatsoever.

What you will use is the repertoire of mental imagery that you have developed for interpreting your dreams, in the course of developing specific psychic skills, and even in everyday experiences. For example, when I first started doing readings, images of shoes spoke volumes to me. Work shoes told me that the person worked hard; shoes in an old-fashioned style told me of their old-fashioned belief system; men's shoes in a woman's reading told me she did work that was usually associated with men, children's shoes for an adult spoke of immaturity, and so forth. As I talked, the shoes "talked" to me by moving and changing. Feet stepping out of shoes that were too tight into comfortable sandals denoted greater freedom. They might walk slow or fast, be new or shabby, and all these descriptions say something about the subject.

A four-leaf clover would indicate good luck, a black cat might mean the opposite. If the clover were far away and moving toward you, the good luck would be coming in, and if the black cat were receding, bad luck would be passing away.

You might develop your own set of symbols to teach to your inner self. Many groups develop their own systems of symbols, such as the symbols in the Tarot cards. Then there are symbols which are universally part of human experience, like a blossoming tree for springtime, with all of its symbolic meanings, or the color green for growth and health.

We practice psychic skills in order to notice the little things that otherwise escape us. We go through exercises, not to become practical, but to become "practiced." It is in the nuances of practice that we can observe the fine and subtle differences that occur in success or failure. These are our teachers.

Through practice we learn to discriminate the value-laden information that comes to awareness from our own programming and acculturation, which is now personal, and the impersonal and clear picture of something outside ourselves. We have learned to categorize everything as good or bad, right or wrong, moral or immoral, and the psyche has no use for any of these particularizations. To the psyche, what is, is. The psyche has been called amoral, without dualistic concepts, outside of the mores of public opinion and belief. And it is into the psyche we must reach for information it can bring to us of the outside world "as it is."

When practicing, learn to drop your morals, values, beliefs, traditions and customs. Through ESP you can get facts. From there, if you attach your personal bias or belief you will distort and make your own what is not yours. The psyche can speak, giving two ideas simultaneously. I will give you an example of how I experienced this. I was teaching a group of students about psychic skills, and decided to give a demonstration to help them accept the reality of psychic skills. I did a "quickie" reading for each, going around the room from left to right. I reached one student, and saw him, in my minds eye, skiing very fast down a difficult ski slope. My impression was that he had had little training in skiing, and was moving so fast the landscape must be just a blur to him. I described this picture that had come into my awareness, and he admitted that recently he had done just that—Skied down a slope for advanced skiers—despite the fact that he had practically no experience in skiing. Sheepishly he admitted to going so fast he saw nothing on the way down. So I was accurate in picking up literal information about an activity of his. But the impression meant more, I felt. I asked him if this was the way he went through life, racing toward his destination without a glance to right or left, not slowing down to "see the daisies" or appreciate the world around him. He admitted this was so. I suggested that one day his inexperience, in an area in which he was forging ahead rapidly, might bring him to grief. A slower pace and more practice in skills of any kind would ensure a safer and more productive life, in my opinion. So the picture I got was of a literal and concrete incident but held more—a significance beyond that event. In fact, the psyche picked that particular activity of his as the best example of meaning which could help him as well as convince him of the reality of ESP.

That same evening, as I moved around the circle of students, I stopped at a girl and focussed my attention on her, open to impressions from her. In came a picture of a hand holding a pill, the other a glass of water. I felt it was aspirin and said so as I described the picture. She looked blank, shook her head negatively, and the student sitting to my right laughed. "It's me you are picking up on," she said. "I've been sitting here with a bad headache, wishing someone would bring me an aspirin with a glass of water." That desire of hers was forceful enough to come between the girl I focussed on and my mind, forcing itself to my attention, and was a good example of "misplacement" which often occurs.

On another occasion, I experienced precognition as I sat quietly with my son to be open to any information which might be helpful to him. After a few moments of focussing on him and emptying my mind of all else, a rapid sequence of events came into awareness. I spoke something like this. "You are advertising for a new occupant for your house, an addition to the group living here, right?" He agreed. "There are three people I see answering the ad, and the third will be the one to take the room if you follow my advice. I see the first as an attractive young man, extroverted and charming, and I advise you to ask him for references before accepting him, which you will want to do." My son objected, saying they had never asked for references before. He felt very uncomfortable with the idea of demanding references.

I continued, "I see your desk with a box of blank checks lying there in the open. Your name is printed on the checks. Is this correct?" He said that it was. "I see this young man taking a pad of blank checks," I went on, "not using them for three years, and then when you do have money in the bank using them to bankrupt you. Even if you don't want to ask this young man for references, don't you think you ought to keep your checkbooks locked up?" He agreed with this motherly advice.

"If you ask this young man for references," I concluded, "all will go well. The second person will not take the room, and the third will be a female, some kind of a teacher. She will be a very nice girl whom you will be glad to have as part of your group here in this house."

My son decided to follow my suggestion. A very nice, personable young man did come and apply. When asked for references he cheerfully gave two, and said that he would call back to learn our decision. The first telephone number was for a diner, where the owner said yes, he came in frequently and drank coffee there, but he didn't know him personally. The woman who answered the second number had never heard of him. He did not call back.

The second applicant changed his mind, and the third was a lovely young art teacher who moved in and contributed much to the group sharing that house.

The point I would like to make with this story is that you should consider the message, not the source, when you get psychic information. The information I was fortunate to be able to pass on to my son was good advice, regardless of where it came from. Don't stand in awe of psychic manifestations; don't belittle the drunk who mumbles words of warning without knowing what he is saying, either. Apply the same criteria you should apply to advice from any source: judge by its quality and content, not by the authority or prestige of the source.

Exercise 1 Psychic Reading (Two People): A reading involves just two people: the reader and the person being read. The person being read is just to relax and listen carefully, making notes on a pad of paper for future reference. The reader is to sit comfortably relaxed in the clear no-mind state which you have been practicing with other skills, and allow images and ideas to flow into awareness. The attention is undirected. As material enters into awareness, the reader must express it verbally to ensure continued flow. Just ramble on about whatever you become aware of, following the current thought and quickly letting go of whatever thoughts were there previously. As you describe what you are aware of, express what it means to you, what feeling experience accompanies it, and any other responses you have. You will find that an idea or image will remain until you have expressed it as completely as you can.

At first the images will be dream-like, and you will have to search for their interpretation as you would in dreams, rather than taking them as literal facts. You have to be willing to give out a lot of material that is incorrect. Among the stream of images will be some nuggets that will encourage you. With time and practice these will come to predominate, the images will become more definite and their interpretations will flow into your mind and out of your mouth with greater freedom and conviction.

At first your turns as reader may only last a few minutes. One tires easily developing a new skill. Stop as soon as you become bored, frustrated, uncertain or tired, and discuss the material you have expressed. Any "hits" or near hits will encourage you, of course, and often you can learn much from your errors. As you remember an image or symbol you might see how you misinterpreted it and thereby improve your understanding of your inner self's symbolic language.

Reverse roles, and have the other person read you while you record the information. Go back and forth a few times, if you want, but don't overdo it. It is a common tendency for students to get excited and pursue a new exercise beyond reasonable limits.

The contents of consciousness that are just out of awareness but easily available we call pre-conscious; what is blocked from awareness we call unconscious. Psychic readers often pick up material blocked from the awareness of their client so they can help them to become aware of it. This is done with the same inner awareness by which we perceive what arises from our own consciousness, except that we are focussing our attention into the consciousness of the other person, where their images and the feelings associated with them lie. The task of the reader is to see them clearly as they are, not through the concepts and beliefs that fill the reader's own consciousness.

To be a vehicle for pure information requires great discipline and dedication. To prevent this from degenerating into your own ego trip, you must practice the clarity of the no-mind state. To prevent it from degenerating into the ego trip of some other being, as in possession and many forms of mediumship, you must take steps such as those described earlier to protect yourself, your client, and the space in which you are working. Surround the whole room with white light, and ask inwardly for protection and guidance.

Remember, the exercises in this chapter are to help you develop your perceptive skills. They should always be done in a relaxed manner. Trying too hard for success in any area will block the flow of perceptions. Now that you have done these exercises to develop your perceptive skills, move on to the next chapter and the exercises on projective skills.

7

Training Your Projective Skills

Projection, like perception, requires a clear, relaxed mind and body. With perception, the idea is to become aware of what is coming in. With projection, the idea is to become aware of what you are sending out. Projection is simply the practice of clearly shaping a mental thought form, filling the thought with an appropriate energy, and then releasing the thought.

The success of projection depends on two key steps. The first is the shaping of the thought. You must know clearly and precisely what it is that you wish to project. The second critical step is releasing. Once you have shaped the thought and energized it, you must release the thought to the subconscious self. It is as if you forget you ever had it. You move on to something else. Sometimes you will think you have let go and yet nothing happens. When this is the case, it is because the thought is being held back on the subconscious level, even though you have released the thought at a conscious level. Thought projection operates on the same principle as a boomerang. You throw it out and after a while it comes back. The boomerang can't return to you if you have never let go of it.

You are already projecting, whether you know it or not. Everyone does. Take a critical look at your environment. What you see is a result of your projections. Thoughts are things. Before the creation of any article, comes the idea or thought of that article. Similarly, before any event or circumstance, someone thought about it as a probable situation. The event or circumstance that has the most mental power invested into it is the one that becomes reality. Become aware that what you think and what you feel are changing the world outside yourself. You can begin to design your life circumstances by consciously designing the thought patterns and the intensity that will accompany them when you project them outward. In developing projective skills, keep in mind that whatever you project outward will be reflected within your environment. Destructive designs will bring destruction to their creator. Constructive designs will result in an harmonious personal environment.

What we fear we often attract to ourselves. If we create a clear picture of the thing we fear, strengthening the picture by repeated imaginings of the feared event, and then fill it with the force of our feelings, what we fear will eventually occur. We create our own disasters! Have you ever wished that what you feared would happen, so you could get over the suspense of waiting? The inner self will get your message and bring it about as rapidly as possible to relieve your discomfort. Watch someone who fears losing a spouse. The jealousy is obvious. Watch his or her behavior. They seem to be working to achieve that loss, and actually they are, although they do not consciously think so. We cannot stand the suspense of an impending loss for long, so our inner self works to bring about a release. Then we cry, "I told you so!" The fear of loss will be relieved by the loss.

You get what you expect. You act and then learn, as a result of your actions, by perceiving what happens. Did you get the desired effect? If not, review your expectations, paying particular attention to the subconscious expectations which may be at odds with the conscious ones. Then try again. Vary the procedure until you get the desired effect.

The purpose of developing your projective skills is to improve your life, to create a better environment for yourself. To work hard to attain mastery of projective skills just to show off, or to demonstrate something useless, is a waste of time. Concentrate your efforts on projections that will have payoffs in practical ways, and that are of benefit to all.

Telepathic Sending

Telepathy involves both perception and projection and requires both a receiver and a sender. Some of us seem to make better receivers, and others of us make better senders. With practice, you can become proficient at both.

Exercise 1 Telepathic Sending With One Another: Decide on someone you want to call you. Remember, it must cause no discomfort or expense to the recipient. At first, select someone who is apt to call you anyway, someone who will find an excuse easily for making the phone call. Write that person's name on a piece of paper. Now close your eyes, lean back and relax. Imagine a scene with that person in it. If you know precisely where the person is, such as office or home, visualize that environment. If you do not know the exact environment, then visualize the person, leaving the details of the background vague. See this person's face. See his or her eyes light up with inspiration and watch the person move to the telephone. See the finger dial your number, and see the telephone receiver held to the ear. Make each sequence clear and concise. See your friend smile and say the word "hello." See yourself pick up your phone and reply. If it helps, write the sequence on paper before you close your eyes to visualize it. Concentrate on this no longer than five minutes. Then let this action drop from your awareness. If, for some reason, you do not get the call within a reasonable length of time, call your friend. It may be that he or she got the message but did not act on it. Ask if your friend was thinking of you at any point in the day. If your friend says yes, ask when and what he or she thought. If your friend thought of you at the time you were projecting, and if the thought was that he or she should call you, then you have been successful. If there was no thought of you, then choose another person to focus on and repeat the exercise.

Exercise 2 Telepathic Sending (Group): This is a simple exercise called the "neck scratcher." Choose someone in the room to be the subject, but do not let this person know it. You can do this at a party, choosing a stranger. All you have to do is to focus on a clear picture of the person scratching his or her own neck, lightly and absend-mindedly. You may visualize a feather tickling the spot. If your projection is successful, the subject will scratch the exact spot. Because no choice has been made by the subject, his or her own inner self will carry out the instructions. The conscious mind may never know what is going on. Of course you will not do anything hurtful, for that would interfere. Try the exercise again with another subject. Then move on to projecting a "beard tug." You can vary this exercise by choosing other parts of the body for the subject to touch.

Exercise 3 Telepathic Sending With One Other: Since emotions are easier to perceive than thoughts, it follows that they are also easier to send. Feeling is a force that colors and influences all forms. Feeling is constantly seeking to express itself in concrete existence. Use this natural urge to send a specific feeling without any form to a loved one. Encouragement, enthusiasm, kindness, compassion, cheerfulness, optimism, love, consideration, self-esteem and hope are a few that you might consider. After choosing your subject, select one definite feeling to send and close your eyes. Picture the subject and the cord that connects you. See this cord clearly. Now imagine a ripple in the cord as the feeling you are projecting travels along it. Like a wave traveling across the ocean, the surface of the cord will ripple in response to the feeling traveling within it. Choose people you feel need a specific feeling in order to bring harmony into their lives. Send the appropriate feeling. However, allow them to reject the feeling if they wish. You can send but you cannot force anyone to receive. Know that your projection can do no harm, but holds the potential for good as it travels to your intended subject. Note the time of your projection, then check with the person to see if he or she had the feeling of the emotion you were sending. Some people simply do not check their emotional states, so they may never realize that what they feel was sent by someone else. Don't be discouraged, just select another subject and try again. Practice this exercise as often as you like.

Exercise 4 Telepathic Sending With One Other: Choose a friend to be a receiver and find a mutually agreeable time to work. Before the appointed time, collect five pictures that you feel will be suitable for the exercise. Each one should evoke specific feelings with you; do not select a picture that you feel wishy-washy about. Out of the five, select one to begin the exercise. Ask your receiver to sit quietly, with as empty a mind as possible. This person may be in another room, another house, or even another town. Focus your attention on the picture you have selected. Look at its form, the lines, the shapes in the picture. Observe the colors and set them into your mental image. Focus on what the picture means to you, and what it might mean to your receiver. Then focus on the feelings the picture evokes within you. As you are sending these feelings, thoughts and images, your receiver will be sitting quietly accepting whatever you are sending. Ask the receiver to write down all the perceptions he or she gets, no matter how bizarre they may seem. Send for only ten minutes and have your partner write for only ten minutes. Have fun and make a game of the exercise. Get together and compare what the receiver has written down with the thoughts you were trying to send and with the picture itself. Try to correlate his or her impressions with your thoughts. For example, while you were mentally projecting the color yellow, your receiver may have written down "banana." The receiver may have simply associated yellow with "banana" and thought that "banana" was your projection, not yellow. Work with the same receiver for a while. Sometimes it takes a few tries to develop psychic rapport with another. You begin to develop a feel for their "mental short-hand," as they do for yours. You will find improvement with practice.

Exercise 5 Telepathic Sending (Solo or Group): Colors have distinct vibratory rates, and specific temperatures, due to the vibratory rate. These two qualities make colors easy to transmit and receive. Select a particular color to transmit. Visualize the color, feel yourself surrounded by it and surround your subject with the color. Mentally select objects that are naturally that color and visualize them. Ask your receivers to write down their perceptions. Spend only two minutes on this exercise, then change the color. Check results after each color. By checking after each try, you will get a better feeling for slight nuances that you might otherwise discount. The perceptions are strongest at the beginning of each try when you are fresh and your subjects are most receptive. Allowing more time per color does not necessarily give you a greater chance of success. In fact, the more time you spend on each color, the more likely that your results will be less than satisfactory. Time tends to diminish success because the conscious mind interferes, for both sender and receiver. Practice this exercise with a variety of receivers so that you can tell whether your sending works consistently or just with one or two receivers.

Exercise 6 Telepathic Sending (Solo or Group): Remove all the jacks, queens, kings and jokers from a deck of playing cards, leaving forty cards. The person you have selected to be a receiver should sit at a table with pencil and paper. Shuffle the cards and then pick one. Study the card and send an image of it to your receiver. The receiver will record on paper what he or she feels the card is. Check the results after each try. If, after three trys, your receiver has gotten none right, vary what you are projecting. If you try to do twenty cards before checking the results, you will have no idea which particular thought projections work and which do not. Repeat the exercise, but only when you are really interested. Boredom will give you a negative score. You may want to start with sending only the color, red or black. Then, when you are satisfied with your results, move on to the numbers plus the colors. Finally, project the suit as well. Try this exercise twenty times, to get statistically valid results. This particular exercise tends not to hold one's attention for very long, so, when you tire of it, stop and move on to another exercise. You can come back to it again later.

Exercise 7 Telepathic Sending With One Other or Group: This exercise is the same as Exercise 6, except that the cards involved are specially designed for ESP. There are two kinds of decks. One is printed in black and white and has twenty-five cards with five symbols: a star, a square, wavy lines, a circle and a triangle. There are five cards of each symbol. The other deck is also composed of twenty-five cards in five groups, but with colors instead of symbols. There are instruction books that come with each of these decks. The exercises in the books are the sending and receiving ones outlined above. If you do not wish to purchase these cards, or if they are unavailable to you, you can make a set of your own. Get some paint chips from the paint store and glue them on index cards or color in circles of color yourself. Make sure you use clear, vibrant color. The stronger the color, the easier it is to transmit and receive. To make the symbol deck, simply take twenty-five index cards and a magic marker, and make each symbol five times, as described above.

Exercise 8 Telepathic Sending with Children: If you are a parent, you can use "telepathic sending" to get a message across to your children. Use mental telepathy when the normal means of communicating are either unavailable or don't seem to be working.

Your children will often ignore your advice, but they can be influenced by silent messages. You can talk to the child in your mind exactly the same way you do with words. Choose a quiet hour at night when the child is asleep and simply repeat your message mentally, directing it to him for several nights in a row.

If your child is needed at home, or is late for dinner and there is no way to reach him or her on the telephone, sending out a mental call to return can produce amazing results.

Sometimes at the end of the day, we regret some of the transactions between us and our children, and wish we could remedy the negative results from them. Sit quietly, by yourself, at a time when the child is asleep, and beam toward his or her mind what you feel. You can ask for forgiveness, or just send reassuring thoughts concerning your love. Or you might want to go into the bedroom and look at your child's sleeping face as you transmit your messages of love and reassurance.

Research about the telepathic rapport between parents and children was done by Dr. Berthold Schwarz of Montclair, New Jersey, and reported in his book *Parent-Child Telepathy*. He found that children frequently act out parents' unspoken fears, transmitted via ESP. He came to believe that what is in a parent's unconscious mind is communicated to the child as, much as if not more than, what is in the conscious mind. He discovered that children can become bathed in the fears of the parents, bombarded by them because of acute sensitivity, and will act out those fears. Dr. Schwarz says that children between the ages of 3 and 7 are particularly sensitive to ESP and will copy a parent's unspoken thoughts regardless of what is being said aloud. Unspoken communications can far outweigh verbal messages.

Group Experiments

When I was young, one of my favorite party games was called "Hot or Cold." In that game, with one guest outside the room, the rest of us would decide on an object for them to find, then call them back in to start the search. We would chant "hot" when they moved toward it, and "cold" when they moved away from it. In that way we steered them, usually successfully, to the object we had chosen. We took turns being the "finder" and had lots of fun and excitement with this game.

When I was in my twenties, three friends and I developed a new form of this old parlor game and called it "Seek, find and do." Again, we took turns being sender and receiver, finding out what each "felt" like and perfecting our skills in both areas.

While the receiver was out of earshot, the rest of us devised a plan that involved steering the receiver from the center of the room, step by step, toward an object, taking that object into his or her hands and then performing some task with it, again step by tiny step.

The senders used three qualities in this experiment. "Willing" the receiver to follow our telepathic directions, keeping a clear image of the next step the receiver was to perform, and desiring that the experiment be performed successfully. We learned that the group had to act in concert with each other, with identical wishes for the experiment to work. In fact, through one disastrous experiment, we found what could happen to an individual who is open to influence and exposed to opposing wills.

After some weeks of practice, we were getting very good at getting immediate results and while Margaret was out of the room, the subject arose of whose will was the strongest, and we decided to experiment on her! The two men, Jim and Bill, would work together and I would try to send her in the opposite direction.

Unaware of what we were up to, Margaret entered the room when we called ready. She shifted into an expectant, receptive state and waited for the urge to move. I was tensely pitting my will against the two men, eager to be the winner, and I am sure they were focussing just as hard to achieve their aim.

We watched, and as we watched, she swayed, first in my direction then in theirs. It was a tense moment for those who knew what was being tried. Her hand went to her forehead, and weakly she said, "I'm confused and dizzy. My head hurts . . . oh, my God, I think I'm going to throw up!"

We immediately ceased, our concern for her sent us to her in consternation as we realized the effect it had had on her. But the worst was yet to come. We led her to the couch and had her lay down. Someone ran for a basin, for she felt too weak to move. She moaned, "My headache is worse! Oh, it hurts!" As I looked, I had my first experience of actually seeing someone turn green. Her pallor was pronounced, with a green tinge to her flesh.

All three of us looked at each other, not daring to tell her what we had done, and not knowing what to do for her. She tossed her cookies, and lay back, looking awful. Finally we got cold, wet cloths to bathe her forehead, and kept murmuring comforting words. Very gradually her color returned, and in about half an hour she was able to sit up and ask "What happened? What were you doing?" We finally confessed, and she was very forgiving as she realized we had no idea it would harm her. That was the last time we four got together, but we had learned two things, two valuable things: mental telepathy works if practiced until it becomes a skill, and the powers of the mind are not to be played with, for they are very real forces.

This experience taught me to always work in unison with my co-workers in any psychic practices, and a heightened respect for the power of the human will. I give you the rule of "No harm to anyone" as an absolute necessity in your practices, and hope you are responsible enough to not misuse your own powers as we did.

For this exercise you need at least three people, preferably more. The subject must leave the room while the rest of the group decides on a target and a procedure for reaching the target.

The "compass needle" form of the exercise is relatively easy and lots of fun. One member of the group is designated as the leader. When the subject is called back by the leader, he or she stands in the center of the room with closed eyes or with a blindfold, whichever seems more appropriate. The group forms a circle around the subject. When the leader silently signals to the group which person in the circle is "it," everyone mentally wills the subject to fall toward that person. When the subject begins to sway in that direction, the group should cease willing and allow the subject to move back into an upright position. Then another person should be selected as the target. The subject should simply stand straight and relaxed, in a receptive "no-mind" state, allowing his or her body to move in the direction of the group's will.

Everyone should take a turn being the subject so that each person learns to be both observer and experiencer. If your group experiences difficulty with this, doubt, skepticism and fear may be getting in the way. It is important that group members have some basic trust for one another. To build trust, and to break possible tension, you might have people take turns actually falling and letting those in the circle catch them. It is important that the circle be small enough—between two and three feet from the subject on all sides.

More complex "willing" exercises must be broken down into simple steps. The group must concentrate on one step at a time, to the exclusion of all other steps, until that part of the action is completed.

No leader is needed for this type of exercise. After the subject has left the room, the group should decide on some clear, definite action as the target. Then they must determine exactly what steps the subject will have to go through to get there after coming into the center of the room.

For example, a sequence of steps might go like this:
1. Turn and face the window.
2. Start walking in that direction.
3. Stop walking and turn to face the bookcase. (If the subject changes direction to avoid a piece of furniture, the group must "steer" by visualizing and focusing on the desired direction.)
4. Start walking in this direction.
5. Stop walking.
6. Lift the right arm. As it is being lifted, move smoothly to the next step.
7. Reach out.
8. Touch a certain book (your target book, clearly visualized).
9. Take the book in your hand.
10. Open the book to page 57.
11. Look at the left-hand page.
12. Read line five.
13. Read line five aloud to us.

The group must be observant and disciplined enough to keep willing one step until it is executed, and then to move on to the next step immediately. The sequence of steps must be clearly understood by each member of the group so that there is no confusion of mental directions to the subject. The directions must be in unison and absolutely identical to have the most impact.

Healing

Psychic, mental or spiritual healing has long been a subject of controversy and ridicule because it is so little understood. For years the media have delighted in calling healers "fakes" due to the number of relapses that occur after a healing has taken place. Before you can understand healing, you have to understand illness. Illness, or dis–ease, is lack of harmony, or ease, in the physical body. This is a result of a lack of harmony in the inner self. The outer state is a reflection of the inner state. When a person is unable to deal with an inner conflict, it is expressed through his or her body. The person will hold on to the illness as long as the inner conflict remains unresolved. When the person gets a healing, he or she may get temporary relief, due to the belief that another can effect a cure, but if the person has not dealt with the underlying issues that have caused the disease within his or her body, the illness will return. People who are out of touch with their emotions and thoughts unconsciously bring a state of illness upon their bodies. The purpose of this is to force them to find the cause of their disease in their belief structure. These people need their illnesses.

When a natural healer tries to help a person who has unconsciously brought the inner conflict to the foreground by attacking his or her own body, the natural healer will only be a temporary solution. The sender, or healer, mentally sends energy to the ill person. How this energy is used is up to the recipient. If the recipient uses the energy as a respite from the dis-ease and looks for the cause within his or her psyche and resolves the conflict, then the energy sent by the healer will appear to have effected a cure. If, however, the recipient still does not make the connection between his or her mental well-being and physical well-being, then the recipient will, rather rapidly, return to the earlier state of imbalance. With any dis-ease, a person is out of balance, and all of his or her energy is used to function from this unnatural state. There is very little left for self-healing. The healer gives the person an extra jolt of energy so that he or she can correct the imbalance. The situation is analogous to jump starting your car. If the battery is low, a charge from another battery will get it going. If you don't take care of your faulty battery, the situation will recur and the battery will need another jump start.

Sending healing energy is a worthwhile project. However, even the best intentions do not always meet with success. Some people have low self-esteem and/or a negative belief system, so they are unable to be receptive to that which is good for them. Others are so defensive that they block everything, good and bad alike. If a healing does not seem to work, do not assume that you are not a competent healer. It is equally possible that the lack of results is the fault of the receiver. A person's lack of receptivity should not deter you from sending healing energy. Whether the person uses the energy or not, it is available. If the person decides, at some point, to resolve personal conflicts, he or she has a reservoir of energy to draw upon.

Healing can be related to any condition which is inharmonious, out of balance or not in a state of perfect health and well-being. This includes the healing of relationships, financial conditions, social conditions or physical ones. Keeping this broad view of the potential work in mind, let us begin with the healing of the physical body.

The diagnosis is the first step. Before you go to work on the case, gather all the information you can find using normal means about the case and review it so that it is impressed into your consciousness. Sit comfortably, relaxed and in private so that you can devote your attention to what you are doing. Tell yourself you want more information about this case and then sit back and let your mind bring into your focussed awareness images, ideas and thoughts. Be aware of these without thinking. Observe carefully what is being brought into focus from your consciousness. Do not interfere with the flow by sending material into your consciousness about what you are perceiving. Avoid random thoughts that will interrupt the sequence of informative ideas and images moving into your awareness to help you heal this particular person or condition. Let it all come to you. This sounds easier than it is in practice, for we all have a tendency to let our attention wander from the task at hand. We are also used to reacting to what comes into our awareness with impulsive action. We need to develop patience as observers, delaying action until later. Practice not reacting although being aware of the desire to react.

Another method of diagnosis to use after you are settled, relaxed and sitting with your eyes closed, is to start with an imagined picture of the patient in your mind's eye. With your attention on this image, allow it to move and create a pantomime that communicates the problem. Be the observer of this. Add whatever you feel will help the progress, such as seating the person in a comfortable chair, or having them stretch out on a bed. Static pictures are difficult to perceive. As a consequence, picture the person moving around, perhaps walking, as in a movie. Whenever you want to examine some detail give a mental order to "stop" the film. Gather all the information you can. Then open your eyes, take up pad and paper and make notes on what you have observed.

Based on whatever information you have, you may safely go ahead and send a healing. Even if your information is incorrect, your efforts will not harm, for each individual has the power to reject and refuse anything entering their personal environment which does not fit the circumstances there. Besides, all you will be sending is "good stuff," images and ideas that help and do not harm.

In the beginning do not try to send healing energy with your telepathic messages. Stick to clear, positive images conveyed with your sincere concern that the condition be healed. Symbolic language, the language of pictures, is the most easily transmitted and the most easily understood by the consciousness of the person who is the target. Use your imagination to find pictures that will convey a message: a needle and thread for sewing up holes, cement for mending bones, vacuum cleaners for cleaning up infection, knives for cutting away obstructions, and other simple, everyday tools that everyone is familiar with. Make movies of simple household tools being used on the person's physical body to clean it, remove something or add something. What is being done here is the creation of a clear message in picture form, transmitted by telepathy to the patient, illustrating what is to be done to heal the dis-ease. It is up to the consciousness of the patient to accept these instructions and proceed with the healing by doing what is necessary. The consciousness in control of the functioning of the body is intelligent and knows how to heal the body and bring it into healthy function. What you are sending is a suggestion that it get busy and do what it knows how to do already.

A case I was given by one member of our healing group was a woman with a severe case of arthritis. I settled back comfortably and imagined a woman in my mind who had twisted fingers, legs and arms. I saw her standing there looking very unhappy. Now I waited for additional information to come into my awareness. I suddenly saw a scene at the supper table. Two men are seated eating, and she is waiting on them. She is hobbling around painfully. I saw them oblivious to her discomfort. The scene disappeared as I understood that she had put their desires before her own for a long time and her own body had become all tied up in knots, as she refused her own self satisfaction while she worked for others. I imagined her in front of me again and my thought to her was that to attain relief she should begin to please herself instead of others. I also used an image of a pair of hands reshaping her fingers, flexing her elbows and massaging all the joints. These two hands reshaped and formed her whole body, as if she were a plastic doll, straightening it up and flexing all the joints so that it moved fluidly. To see if my directions were clear, I instructed my consciousness to allow that figure to move for me so that I could see if the results were good. A smile lit up the face of the image in my mind and the arms and legs performed for me, dancing about in the space in my awareness. That concluded my work on the case except for a personal message I sent with my co-worker. After working on the case I asked my co-healer if the subject did, in fact, sacrifice her own interests for those of her own family. When the answer was yes, I then suggested she relay this message from me. Start catering to yourself and stop catering to them. Let them take care of themselves and ask them to return some of the good care you have given them.

Exercise 1 Healing With One Other: Ask someone who does not feel well to be the recipient of the healing. Someone with a tension headache is a good subject to start with, because tension is usually temporary. Ask the person to take several deep breaths, to relax, and to be open to the healing energy you are going to send. Clear your mind, and from your own quiet and centered place, direct energy to your hands until you feel them grow warm and begin to tingle. Then, place your hands on the spot that needs the healing, directing the energy through your hands to the recipient. Visualize the muscles and blood vessels relaxing and mentally send the tension away. When you feel that you have directed enough energy (a few minutes should do), remove your hands. Wash your hands immediately so that you wash out of your aura any of the negative vibrations you may have inadvertently picked up. This is particularly important if you are going to heal someone else right away, because you would not want to pass one person's negativity on to another. If there are no immediate results, do not worry. The body may need some time to use your energy to rebalance. Ask the person to be honest and inform you of any change.

Exercise 2 Healing (Group): Gather together a group of eight or so people who would like to do a healing. Form a circle and place the person who is to be the recipient of the healing in the middle. Have everyone relax, clear their minds, and enter the no-mind state. Then, as a group, visualize a circle of white light enclosing the group. Then all visualize a circle of purple, a healing color, then a circle of green, the color of peace and tranquility. When the circle of light and energy is strong, direct it toward the recipient until that person is enshrouded in light, peace and healing. Keep directing this energy for a few minutes, while you envision the ache or pain leaving the subject's body. Visualize the unbalanced part of the sufferer's body as whole and healthy and affirm perfect health for that person. After a few minutes, stop and quietly let the energy recede. Ask the receiver if he or she felt anything during the exercise. Ask the receiver to be honest. Most people, in this particular situation, will tell you what you want to hear. Get a very clear reading from the receiver as to whether he or she felt anything or not. If not, try the exercise a second time. If you get the same results, try a new receiver.

Exercise 3 Healing (Group): This exercise is like Exercise 2, except that we introduce the "laying on of hands." After the energy has been raised by the group, have the members place their hands on the recipient. This will give a more direct transfer of energy. Observe the results. Often times, the recipient will flush from the infusion of so much energy at once. Swelling can be decreased very rapidly with this group action. A few minutes is all that is necessary. In our group, we did this exercise to one of our members, who had a swollen jaw from a tooth extraction. A hour after we finished with the exercise, his swelling had almost disappeared.

Exercise 4 Healing (Solo or Group): This exercise is called absentee healing. Alone or with a group, mention aloud the name of the person to whom you wish to send the healing energy. Visualize this person as whole and healthy. Mentally, go over the whole body and direct your energy to the particular part that you feel needs special attention. You do not have to know the individual to do this. If you do this with a group, it is helpful if the namer of the recipient knows where the trouble lies in the body. The group can choose not to know what the ailment is at the beginning, and at the end of the healing each can try to identify where the ailment was located. This exercise can be done at any time and in almost any circumstance.

You can heal any condition in your own life with which you are unhappy. First you must gain from your own consciousness a clear picture of the situation and the source of the difficulty. Your feelings about it must rise into awareness in order to be confronted and healed. Realize that you are the original cause of all your circumstances by what you have accepted into your own organism. This will give you the power to change anything you want.

Think of experiences as being like food that enter the system. Food comes into our mouth and goes down into the digestive system. The body is still distinct from the food that has come into it. But then a process goes to work: digestion. The food is digested so that it becomes part of the body, no longer a separate "thing." The food and the body are now one. Our consciousness is cluttered with undigested experiences that have never become truly part of us. These experiences, swallowed whole, include ideas, beliefs and concepts that can live side by side but in conflict with one another. Very often these things that lie heavy in our consciousness are "at one" with someone else, or society at large. For instance, any conviction that some relative of mine had and passed on to me lodges in my consciousness. For some reason I never made it my own, although I kept it. It is still "one with my relative" and may be in opposition to my best interests. As long as I keep it in my consciousness it will cause trouble and disharmony.

A good example is attitudes about money. From my early Sunday School training a belief about money was deposited in my consciousness. Money is evil. Poverty is virtuous. It is bad to be rich. Then I went out into society and found that social approval was given to those who made money, those who had money, those who had many possessions. These experiences were also absorbed into my consciousness where they went to war with my religious beliefs. What to do? I needed healing for my economic well being. If I had a surplus of money, I felt guilty. If I had too little, I felt awful. There was no harmony or feeling of well-being for me in any economic circumstance. How to heal it?

I sat down one day, got comfortable and closed my eyes. I imagined the church of my early childhood training. I saw myself go into that church and confront a person in there who represented the church beliefs to me. I held out my closed hand, pretending I held those long ago taught beliefs about money in them. I had the person hold out his hand and then I placed my hand over it putting back all I'd been given. Smiling, he accepted. The message to my unconscious was to return something to the original owner that I had been harboring for a long time. It did not belong to me. This freed me to gain whatever amount of money I wanted to get any my level of affluence I might choose.

Psychokinesis

Psychokinesis is the ability to move objects with mental energy. Instances of psychokinesis tend to be rare, due to the commonly held belief that moving objects with mental energy is impossible. However, Uri Geller[5] became a most controversial figure, due to his psychokinetic abilities. He demonstrated to millions that metal can be bent by the mind alone. His bending of spoons, forks and keys stunned millions of TV viewers. When Geller performed his feats on BBC television, many viewers found themselves bending metals in their own homes, unconsciously!

This unconscious manipulation of mental energy, affecting objects outside the individual, is clearly evident in the so-called "lucky" gamblers who shoot dice. These gamblers talk to the dice, they focus their desires on the dice and then they "shoot" the dice or throw them and get the desired number. They appear to be incredibly lucky. However, look closely at what really happens. The gambler has no preconceived idea about the impossibility of shooting the number he or she wants. The gambler really cares about the outcome of the throw, and focuses attention on the number he or she *needs* to win. Then, as the gambler throws the dice, he or she lets go mentally of the desire and waits expectantly for the outcome. Unconsciously, the gambler has used mental energy to affect the outcome of the throw. His or her success lies in an ability to let go of the desire after focusing attention on it. If the gambler kept trying to will the dice after throwing them, his or her success would be blocked. The releasing of the intent is critical, so that the subconscious can take over and affect the outcome. This dice-throwing phenomena has produced some interesting experiments in ESP research conducted at Duke University.

The researchers had volunteers try to influence falling dice. They found that their success was much higher than the probability indicated by statistics. Continued effort with the dice caused the scores to drop. As I have pointed out, boredom is the biggest cause of declining results. Feeling, intent or desire is a very necessary ingredient for success.

In his book, *The Roots of Coincidence* (Random House, 1973), Arthur Koestler states that there is no such thing as chance, only laws and rules of the universe with which we are not yet acquainted. Let us uncover some of these unknown laws governing energy with the exercise below.

Exercise 1 Psychokinesis (Solo): Place a lighted candle in front of you, far enough away so it will not be affected by your breath. Make sure that the room you are working in has no air currents to interfere with the flame. Block up any drafts, close the doors and windows and otherwise

---

[5]Uri Geller is a well-known practitioner of psychokinesis. For more information, read *Uri Geller: My Story* (Warner Books, 1976) and *Uri Geller* by Andrija Puharich.

prepare the place thoroughly so that the candle flame burns straight and upright. When all is ready, sit quietly staring at the flame, willing it to move sideways until it forms a right angle with the unburned portion of the candle. Visualize the desired result as you are directing your energy. Staring is not necessary, so do not forget to blink. Concentrate your energy on the flame until it bends to your will. Concentration is not effort, it is focussed attention. Effort tenses your body and skin and will only serve to hinder the release of your energy. Once you have bent the flame, release the energy and watch the flame resume its upright position.

Exercise 2 Psychokinesis (Solo): Put enough water in a shallow bowl so that the bowl is two-thirds full. Tap water will do. Place the bowl on a table and sit facing it. As you sit there, focus your attention on the water. Let your mind be calm and clear, then visualize the water swirling in the bowl. See the force making it swirl faster and faster. Create this clearly in your mind. Then, *release the thought.*

Let me tell you a story of a student of mine, who was experimenting with this exercise. He did the exercise correctly, right up to the releasing part, but as he stared at the water, it did not move. The phone rang. With a sigh, he rose from the chair feeling like a failure, but determined to try again after answering the phone. On his return, he found that a lot of the water had splashed out of the bowl, all over the table. At least half of the water was now outside the bowl. What had happened? When he left to answer the phone, his attention was distracted and he released the desire to move the water. Once he had let go of his own energy, his energy moved out as directed and gave him the result he desired. He was not there to see it, only the effects of his energy on his return. The interruption forced him to release the thought because he had to direct his attention to something else. This is a clear illustration of the problem of releasing. We may *think* we have released a thought, only to find out later that we really haven't. This exercise with the water is excellent for becoming aware of the releasing problem. Everyone can move water psychically. Once you have mastered this, other projective exercises will be much easier.

Exercise 3 Psychokinesis (Group): Prepare a surface that dice will bounce but not slide on; for example, a blanket spread on a table. Provide each member of the group with a pencil and some paper so that each person can keep his or her own score. You will also need four dice and a container.

A member will throw the four dice at one time, noting the number on each die as a separate score. Before throwing the dice, have each person in the group write down the number he or she desires to throw. (Remember each die is a separate score, so the numbers picked can only range from one to six.) Group members will write down their desired number on the left side of their score sheet. Then each will take a turn at throwing the dice. Each member will count the number of times the chosen number turns up and record this score on the right side of the page. He or she will choose a second number and throw again. Each person should get six turns. After the sixth throw, the participants will add up their scores. Out of the six throws of four dice, laws of probability indicate that one should get a total of four hits. This is without using any psychic power; it is pure chance. The object of this exercise is to do better than chance. Add up your score and subtract four. The remainder is an indicator of your ability to use psychokinesis. The accompanying sample score sheet shows you how the exercise works.

SAMPLE SCORE SHEET

Target Chosen	No. of Hits
4	1
6	3
2	1
5	2
1	0
3	2

9 total number of hits

subtract 4

you had 5 more than chance expectation

If, after doing the perceptive and projective exercises, you feel that you are having trouble developing your psychic skills, do not give up. It may be that you have some subconscious blocks you are unaware of. Spend some time with the next chapter on beliefs, then go back and do the exercises again. You will see a marked improvement.

Exercise 4 Psychokinesis (Group): Hang up a string of bells and have the whole group focus their attention simultaneously on the string of bells, willing them to move, injecting them with motion-energy from each personal will, so that activity among the bells will produce some sound.

Hang a pendulum from the ceiling and seat the group around it, not touching it, but keeping their eyes focussed on it during the experiment. No physical contact, only eye contact. Again, the group should will it to move, visualizing a wave of energy moving out from the group which can set it in motion. If the group is seated in a circle, it is wise to determine before hand what kind of motion is desired. Clockwise circling or a back and forth movement, for instance. If back and forth, make a clear demonstration of the exact diagonal it is desired to swing in.

The principle elements in mind over matter practices are a firm and clear plan, and an intense desire and firm will for it to happen. Each person's will, mind and feeling must be in accord, and the design of the practice clearly outlined.

Exercise 5 Levitating an Object (Group or Solo): Place a light object such as a matchstick, a plastic coin or a toothpick on a bare table. Sit down, do your breathing and relaxation exercises, and then focus your attention on the object. Feel its weight mentally.

Let your awareness become more focussed and deeper as you mentally feel the weight of the object lessening, getting lighter and lighter. Breathe more deeply as you experience the object losing its weight. This will tend to equalize the gravity force on it with a greater force coming from within you. As it becomes lighter, begin giving it a firm command to rise. Your will will be done, if your will is firm and your imagination clear and well-developed. Try other objects such as a bottle cap. Try this experiment often, and eventually the object will rise in the air. The first time it happens it may distract your attention and immediately go back down. You can learn to keep your attention focussed, willing it to rise higher and higher. This has been done, and you can do it too, if you wish. If your desire to do it is strong enough, and your determination deep enough to keep you practicing until it happens.

When I was teaching psychic skills, one of my students decided he would like to develop the skill of psychokinesis—the ability to move objects with the mind alone. Harold decided to work with a compass needle, and asked me how to proceed.

We first discussed what human need that accomplishment would satisfy, for I have found this factor absolutely essential to the nervous system that performs the feat. We determined that there is a general public need "to know" about psychic skills in order that they can utilize them, and he then started to practice in his dormitory room every chance that he had. He made sure he had a witness to these practice sessions, and eventually the witnesses testified he was able to move the needle slightly from its northward pointing position. He was jubilant, and continued with renewed zeal.

His next experiment used a ping pong ball, on the basis that we practice with the easiest, not the most difficult object to move. He concentrated his focus of both mind and eye on the ping pong ball, willing it to roll away from him or toward him. He became very intense about achieving this performance. One day his roommate was serving as witness, and they both observed that the ball actually disappeared for a moment from their steady gaze! They rushed to me for an explanation, but I could only surmise that the intensity of energy that reached the ball must have changed its rate of vibration, like a fan moves from slow to fast, disappearing from our gaze because of its speed of rotation. The ball was still on the table, but its vibrational speed had been increased to the point of invisibility to human eyes. At the sight of it disappearing, Harold's concentration was changed, and the ball quickly appeared again to their sight, reverting to its normal vibrational frequency.

Psychic Photography

Psychic photography is as old as cameras, yet very little is known about it. It takes many different forms, usually spontaneous. Back in the days of photographic studios and big cameras with hoods for photographers to creep under to take the picture, some professionals had a lot of difficulty with "spoiled" film. Instead of getting a nice picture of the posed subject, they were getting streaks of light or superimposed pictures of people who weren't there! It was finally realized the effects were created from the unconscious of the photographer and recognized as a phenomena which could be used profitably.

The early spiritualist camps which drew hundreds of people to their summer sessions were fertile grounds for these talented photographers. Most attending wanted their picture taken with their friends, or alone, to see what would manifest in the final print.

My Aunt Lizzie gave me one of these photographs which I treasure. There she sits, with her friends, smiling happily, and in the atmosphere above them are a number of faces, some of whom were identified by the sitters, others still unknown. She treaured this photograph for years, and knew I would care for it as much as she did. I've seen others too, when I have met friendly people who own them.

Other people have had spontaneous results with photograhs which are not easily explained. Others have deliberately tried to get photographs of invisible beings or mental projections.

Two friends of mine went to Chicago to a spiritualist convention a few years ago, and attended a class for psychic photography. The medium who presided over this class was well-known for being able to get results from pieces of printing paper pressed to the solar plexus or forehead of those he sat with in a dark seance room as they meditated under his instruction. One result that came out well was an experiment on mental visualization to imprint the paper. My friend pictured a safety pin, and I saw the result. A sharply defined white safety pin against a black background. My other friend, a young lawyer, was surprised at one of the sessions to find faces on his paper. He recognized them as relatives, now dead, but known by him during his boyhood years.

There is the famous case of Ted Serios written up by Dr. Jules Eisenbud with many startling prints reproduced in the book. Dr. Eisenbud's research with Ted covered about three years and uncovered some very odd things. Ted would place a cap over a polaroid camera and then focus on the lens when the camera was loaded, usually producing a picture. Most of them were scenes. The one I remember best is of a Chicago storefront. The building is there today, and quite recognizable in this picture. But the picture shows it with a large sign on it which had been removed over twenty years ago. *The World of Ted Serios* is a fascinating book if your interest is aroused by psychic photography. It won't tell you how it is accomplished, for that was not discovered, but it proves to any reader that it does happen.

Perhaps the chemicals used on photographic paper are very sensitive to the radiation that issues in a focussed manner under the human will.

A small group at the University of Connecticut tried the experiment of numbering pieces of unexposed photographic printing paper, meditating on them in the dark, and then wrapping them up to be developed later. I have those prints. The only odd thing that occurred is that some are absolutely black, some came out very white and some mixed. And all were held in the same atmosphere, a sealed room where no light could be detected. We ended up just puzzled. No answers.

Exercise 1 Polaroid Psychic Photography (Group or Two People) This exercise requires at least two people, but more can participate. A loaded polaroid camera is needed. The subject is the person who will visualize a picture, projecting it to the center of her or his forehead. The photographer is the person who will hold the camera and place it about one inch away from the forehead of the subject on the signal from the subject that he or she is ready to concentrate with intensely focussed attention. The subject should take time to prepare, relaxing and getting comfortable. The desired picture should be clearly visualized, including components of meaning and feeling within the objective form of the picture.

Exercise 2 Solar Plexus Photography (Group or Solo): This experiment must be done in a completely dark room, for photographic printing paper is used. If this is not available in small squares or oblongs, someone should use a dark-room to cut it into 3x5 or similar size pieces for the practice. These pieces are kept in a light-barrier envelope until you are ready to use them. The doors and windows of the room should be sealed with tape, if necessary. No leakage of light can be allowed or the experiment may not work. A red light bulb can be lit if needed. Each person is supplied with a pencil. As they are seated in a circle around the dark room, give each one a piece of photo paper. It will have a slick side and a textured side, to the touch. On the textured side the participant will write his or her name.

The participants must first relax and center, entering a no-mind state, and then clearly visualize the picture each desires. When this visualization is clearly formulated, including elements of personal feeling and meaning, it is ready to "photograph." When ready, each participant should press the slick side of the paper against his or her solar plexus, maintaining the clear focus of the picture for about ten minutes. All must be silent, so that there will be no distractions. At the end of ten minutes, collect the exposed pieces of paper and seal them in the protective envelope again. Then take the pieces of paper to a person or firm who will develop them and return them.

Alternatively, have two trays of solution prepared in the dark room, one tray of developer and the other of fixative, with a bowl of fresh water beside each tray. Each person may develop his or her own picture. Slip the paper into the developer until a picture is seen, rinse it, then drop it into the fixative. Let it stay there until all the prints have been developed. Then wash them all and lay them out to dry and be viewed. During this process, light a red bulb so you can see what you are doing; it will not affect the paper.

8

Beliefs And Your Psychic Development

The success or failure you had with the exercises in the preceding two chapters hinged on your subconscious beliefs about your ability to do the exercises. Positive beliefs about your psychic development will enhance your ability to do the exercises; negative beliefs will impede your ability. For example, if you approached the exercises with the attitude that they were fun and that the "doing" of the exercises would produce the expected results, then that is precisely what you got, results. If, on the other hand, you approached the exercises with the belief that developing your psychic skills would be difficult, then the results, or lack of results that you got reflect that preconceived idea of difficulty. Your results are frustrated. Actually, you are the one who is frustrated,—by your own negative beliefs, not by the results. The results reflect your own belief system.

The trouble with beliefs is that we so often mistakenly call them facts. Most people find it difficult to separate beliefs from facts. By confusing beliefs and facts we color future life experiences by our preconceived ideas about life before we actually experience it. In other words, the preconceived ideas and beliefs we have in any area condition our success or failure there. Positive beliefs assist success; negative beliefs block success. What is worse is that the negative beliefs we hold form psychological barriers between our conscious and subconscious selves, disrupting our energy flow and making success either limited or impossible. Most of the time we are unaware that a belief we hold is negative or limiting; we are only aware that a certain area of our life is not working well. Instead of looking to our inner self to see what we really believe, we tend to look outside ourselves for external causes for our troubles. Often we are unaware of what we really believe.

Our subconscious minds are filled with attitudes, beliefs and ideas about reality. They are not facts about reality, only what we believe about reality. We confuse ourselves by accepting belief as a fact. For example, if you have been told since you were a child that there is no such thing as telepathy, and if you have accepted the statement as true, then your inner self will believe that telepathy does not exist. This is a belief about reality, not a statement of fact about reality. Yet because you accept the belief as true, you perceive it as a fact about reality rather than a belief about reality. As a consequence, your inner self will continue to act as though telepathy were impossible. When you attempt to develop your telepathic ability you will fail, since success would contradict the belief about the impossibility of telepathy which you have accepted and given to your inner self as a fact about the universe.

The inner self is very concerned with your survival and well-being. It works to ensure that your actions and responses correspond with reality. But where does it get its ideas about reality?

Most of the beliefs or ideas we hold as adults are a conglomeration of other people's beliefs. They need to be re-examined. It is important to realize that just because someone has told you something is so, does not necessarily mean it is so. We allow other people to hypnotize us into their way of thinking. Very few of the beliefs we hold about the world are facts, and very few of the beliefs we hold are based on our personal experiences of the world. Most of our beliefs are someone else's version of reality.

Negative beliefs can impede your success in any area of your life, not just psychic development. It is better to enter into any experience with an open mind, a mind free of preconceived ideas. Think about the word "preconceived." What does it mean? When we "preconceive," we formulate ideas and beliefs about an experience or event *before* it has taken place. In other words, before we have any first-hand knowledge. Would you eat chocolate pudding if you decided beforehand it was going to taste awful? Probably not. But why deny yourself the experience of finding out for yourself what chocolate pudding actually tastes like. Our culture continually bombards us with preconceived ideas and beliefs about everything we do. Whenever you hear the word "should" it will likely. be followed by someone's preconceived idea about how things "should" be. Pay attention to your own "shoulds." You don't have to reinvent the wheel, but do examine carefully what other people tell you is the truth. More often than not they are telling you a belief, something they believe to be the truth. Beliefs permeate all levels of our culture, and the most fundamental ones are the most dangerous.

One of the most pervasive beliefs shared by nearly all Western cultures is the belief that nature is our enemy, and must be combatted constantly. This Western view of the division between man and nature lies at the base of our scientific heritage. Allopathic medicine, is based on this theory, and "attacks" natural events like childbirth and fever (which fights infection naturally) with drugs and surgery. Allopathic doctors do not believe the body and the mind are homeostatic (self-righting) mechanisms. They do not believe the body is capable of healing itself. They have convinced almost all Westerners of this belief. We have become neurotic about our body's ability to heal itself. Our doctors have convinced us of the absolute necessity of outside interference. We have been hypnotized by their beliefs. Homeopathic medicine takes the opposite view, realizing that nature is our ally. Homeopathic medicine uses healing methods and herbs that are natural to the body's chemistry, rather than synthetic. Yet, despite the success of homeopathic medicine, doctors in this country still believe that nature and our bodies are hostile toward us. For them disease is normal and health is abnormal.

In *Parapsychology and the Nature of Life, Harper and Row, 1977,*John L. Randall deals with the two opposing theories of nature and man. If we hold the view that nature is hostile to us, it follows that the natural self within is our enemy, and must be controlled. Fearing the natural self, our culture has set up logic as the only method of operation. We teach our children to use only logic in problem solving. By the time they leave our educational system, they no longer trust their natural impulses and intuitions. They do not trust themselves (just as doctors do not trust the body to heal itself). They come out programmed with a lot of "shoulds" which repress their natural spontaneity and their ability to approach life openly.

The unnatural barrier which has been erected between us and our natural selves, by the erroneous concept that nature is our enemy, can be melted away. Whatever our age, we can create a new world view. If we replace our negative belief about nature with the positive belief that nature is our friend and works for us not against us, the unnatural barrier will dissolve. Our intuitive self will function in harmony and in cooperation with our logical self.

To restore the wholeness of personality is to restore our potential for psychic communion. Knowledge that the world outside ourselves is but a reflection of the world within permits us to develop trust of our natural self, of others and of the universe.

By developing harmony within, one can learn life's lessons easily. If one is at odds with one's self, then the lessons of the universe are confusing and misunderstood. Because most people in our culture are at odds with their natural, nonlogical self, they misunderstand the cues, or feelings, the natural self sends us for corrective action in the future.

Possibly the most misunderstood cue sent by the natural self to the reasoning self is guilt. Natural guilt is built into every living thing. In animals, natural guilt manifests itself as instinct, keeping indiscriminate killing in check. In the wild state, animals only kill to eat; never for sport, never over words and rarely their own kind. In human beings, natural guilt is triggered when we have transgressed some natural, or universal, law. Since we are mere mortals, it would be foolish for us to expect to know all the ways of the universe. Natural guilt is nature's way of saying, "Don't do that again." It is simply the natural self saying to the reasoning self, "Gee, that action didn't make us feel so good, so let's not do it again." Natural guilt causes disharmony within parts of the self, so that the reasoning self looks at the action and vows not to do it again.

Natural guilt has nothing to do with punishment. Punishment is a cultural concept. The association between guilt and punishment comes from the erroneously held belief that humankind is perfect. This "illogical logic" holds that men and women are perfect, yet have managed to transgress some universal principle, evident by guilt within the self, then they must be punished for their fall from grace. Yet, if one really perceived the universe, one would realize that life is a learning experience for the soul, and that humankind is ever in the state of becoming. When viewed from this perspective, natural guilt becomes a teacher. We must change our action in order to alleviate the guilt. Once the action is changed, we are more in accord with universal principles, and the guilt dissolves until the next time we need a mental nudge to reconsider our actions.

This confusion in our thinking and beliefs about human perfection and the need to be punished for a fall from perfection has cast guilt, a natural learning tool, in a villainous role. Guilt pervades our society. Not natural guilt, our learning tool, but misplaced guilt tied to the widely accepted belief that human beings *should* be perfect. Our incorrect beliefs have so corrupted our feeling of natural guilt that we feel guilty for the wrong things, and seek punishment to alleviate the guilt. Often people actually desire punishment, for this is what they *feel* and *believe* they deserve, instead of seeking to change the behavior that produced guilt originally.

In developing your psychic skills, it is imperative to look carefully at your beliefs about reality. Remember, these are only beliefs, which can be changed, and not facts about reality which you cannot change. If you can separate what you believe from what you think is a fact about reality, you will be able to eliminate a lot of your misplaced guilt. Negative beliefs about the existence of psychic ability will impede your progress; and negative beliefs about your own self-worth can produce an enormous amount of misplaced guilt.

Can you figure out why? Think carefully about the next few sentences. Your beliefs condition your life experience. Feeling like a failure attracts failure into your life. Fear of success is always accompanied by its counterpart, the desire to fail. Why would you want to fail? The desire to fail comes from a deep-seated feeling of unworthiness. If one is somehow nevertheless successful, contradicting the belief in one's own worthlessness, the result is intense distorted guilt. (How can one be successful, if one is unworthy?) In an attempt to alleviate this stressful condition, the subconscious will set up a failure, so that the self can be returned to the original position of unworthiness, while believing in human perfection.

If you hold contradictory beliefs, and we all do, the results will be reflected in your life. By using the techniques I explain here, you can begin to resolve some of these conflicting concepts and belief.

Reprogramming

Reprogramming is a technique by which we repattern our old thought and behavior patterns into a more beneficial system. Reprogramming works best if you can learn to view the past events of your life as if they were on film. In your head you simply play the tape of the event that you want to reprogram, and then rewrite the script. The same holds true for beliefs.

Exercise 1 Reprogramming (Solo): Before attempting to reprogram your beliefs, run through the relaxation exercises I discussed in Chapter 2. After attaining a relaxed state, let your mind drift. While drifting, ask your consciousness to bring forth an incident that has produced anxiety or fear in your life. Let your thoughts flow along with the recall of the event for a few moments. View your life as a movie, and rewind the film to some past life experience. Ask your conscious self to replay the entire event again, this time in slow motion. Be very observant of all your emotions and feelings as the incident unfolds. Undoubtedly the event you are recalling will have been one that you took very seriously. Now, begin to rerun the event again, in slow motion, but every few frames, silently say "stop" and insert some other picture, a change of feeling, a change of action or reaction. The inserted frame will now become a permanent part of your memory about this event.

Here is a real life illustration. A student of mine had a tremendous fear of snakes. She feared snakes for so long that the original cause of this fear was lost to her memory. Her fear was so severe, it limited her in venturing anyplace that snakes possibly might be. By using the film technique, she was able to move back to a time in her life when she was about six years old. She saw herself running through a pasture and stepping on a nest of baby snakes, barefoot. She shuddered as she remembered the incident. Running the film again, in slow motion, she found it difficult to get beyond her lifted foot, just before stepping on, so we paused there. She inserted a new version of what happened. As she lifted her foot, she imagined that she looked down into the snake nest; one snake had purple and white stripes, one was cross-eyed, one stuck out its tongue at her! She made the event humorous. Very slowly, we changed the movie in her head so that her foot came down just outside the nest. Her other foot came up along the other side, as she continued to look at these tiny, baby snakes which were harmlessly funny. Then she finished the reel, and let herself run across the pasture.

Using this as an example, vary the technique so it will work with your own memories and problems. Change them until, when recalled, they include the new image. When you can rerun the event so that only the new pleasant images appear where the painful ones were previously, then you will have removed a limiting factor from your life.

Exercise 2 Reprogramming (Solo): Using the same technique described in Exercise 1, you can also replace beliefs that you have absorbed from others. We all have internalized instructions from other people on what we should believe, feel and fear. Few of us have bothered to change any of these instructions and beliefs when they contradict our own life experiences.

For this exercise, instead of an incident, use a belief you have about reality. Try and remember where you got the belief. Was it from an actual life experience, or was it from another person? Run the movie in your head until you locate the first time you became aware of the belief. Nine times out of ten you will find that the beliefs you have are "shoulds" that someone else has told you: "If you do such and such, you *should* feel guilty." When you come upon a section of your life movie where someone is saying "should" to you, listen and observe carefully what follows the "should." If the idea or attitude is one that causes anxiety in you, or in some way limits your potential growth, then insert in your movie a new scene, one of you giving the attitude back to the person who gave it to you in the first place. Symbolize the belief or attitude by an object, make a "gift" out of it, and reenact the drama—a scene in which you give the "gift" back to the sender. For instance, in your movie, you hear your mother saying that anyone who believes in ESP is bad. Imagine that this belief is symbolized by a gigantic gift box tied with a big red bow, and then see yourself handing it to your mother. Imagine the scene as happy and carefree, with your mother accepting the "gift." Remember, this is your movie and you can script the scene any way you want. Then, repeat out loud, if possible, "The belief about_____(or fear of_____) has left me and has gone back to where it came from. I am relieved of it and need not believe or fear it any longer."

Another technique for exploring one's personal programming uses the pendulum. The pendulum is guided by your autonomic nervous system and is an excellent way to get at beliefs that we have accepted as facts. A review of the pendulum technique outlined in Chapter 5 will refresh your memory.

Exercise 3 Reprogramming (Solo): Make a list of your attitudes and beliefs about yourself. Start with the statement, "I am _____ ." Set a timer for ten minutes and keep writing until the timer rings. Write whatever comes into your head. *Do not censor your thoughts.* You will find many contradictions such as I am smart, I am dumb, and so on. Don't be bothered by them; just keep writing. After making your list, review it, and then cross out anything that is a statement of fact. In my case, for example, "I am female," is a statement of fact. I am stupid, smart, intelligent, dumb, sensitive, uncaring, fat, skinny, ugly, beautiful and so on are all beliefs about yourself. The only facts you will find will be clearly specific; I am female, blue-eyed, brown-haired. The rest of the words are relative terms and therefore not facts. They are matters of opinion. They are only beliefs about yourself that are reinforced by our cultural standards. The good thing about beliefs is that they can be changed. But first, it is necessary to find out how deeply you hold a belief. Draw a straight line across a piece of paper with a ruler. Using a compass or a round object such as a bowl or coffee can, draw a semicircle above this line. With the ruler, divide it into three equal pie-shaped sections. Where the points of the pie-sections meet in the center of the line, draw a small circle. Finally label the three sections, around the edge of the semicircle: the one on the left is "light," the one in the center is "medium" and the one on the right is "heavy."

Take your pendulum, and, using this diagram, find the depth to which each belief has become fixed in your consciousness. Hold the pendulum over the small circle, the neutral zone, and read each item out loud, one at a time. As the pendulum moves, write down where each belief registers on the intensity scale. When you have finished, rewrite the list, separating the beliefs into the three intensity categories. Carefully study these three lists and you will get a clear picture of your social self that was in large measure created by internalizing other people's attitudes and beliefs about you.

See if you can identify the source of each belief you have written down about yourself. Did someone say to you, "You're so clumsy, you never do anything right!" all the time? If so, the belief, I am clumsy, really belongs to that person, not you. The person you mentally hear saying the same thing about you that you have written down as a belief about yourself will be the person who implanted that belief in you. The person may have done this to manipulate you so that you became the version of yourself that that person could control. By reviewing and analyzing your list of beliefs, you can become independent of them. Discard the beliefs that limit you. "I am stupid" is a limiting belief. "I am intelligent" is an expanding and positive belief. Retain the beliefs that are positive and constructive; erase the ones that are negative and limiting. Begin to recreate your social self in the image you desire to be.

Exercise 4 Reprogramming (Solo): Take your original list from the exercise above, and rewrite it in terms of the contradicitions you find there. For example, group together I am dumb with I am smart; this is a contradiction. Go through the entire list sorting out the contradictions. In some areas, you will find no contradictions. You may have written down, I am pretty, or handsome. If you find no contradictory statement on your list, then you have no tension within yourself about your appearance. Study the areas in which you find the contradictions. Then study the areas in which you have no contradictions.

If you look at your list of contradictions carefully, you will find that it is in these areas of your life that you are least successful. By holding contradictory beliefs, you, in effect, stalemate yourself and your success in that area. The areas in which you do not have contradictory beliefs are the parts of your life in which you enjoy most of your success but only if these beliefs are positive ones. If the noncontradictory beliefs held are negative ones, then in these areas of your life you will be even less successful than you are in the areas in which you hold contradictory beliefs. A belief held without contradiction is a very strong belief, whether positive or negative. Make sure yours are positive ones.

Exercise 5 Reprogramming (Solo): Using the pendulum and the intensity scale, write down all your beliefs about one of the following: the universe, time, cause and effect, what you fear, what you like, love, your friends, your parents, your brothers and sisters, your mate, money, social status, and your home. Add topics of your own. Pick one category a day and give yourself ten minutes of writing time. Study your lists carefully. Before you cross off anything as a fact, be sure you can validate it by your own personal life experience. If you cannot validate your fact by your own experience, leave it as a belief for the time being. There are many universal laws that are unknown to us, and there are many laws that we only partly perceive; thus we have the "whole" of it wrong. Do not be so willing to accept the standard, or scientific, view of reality. Remember, for centuries people *believed* that the world was flat and accepted that belief as a fact about the world, until someone was willing to try out this belief in a real life drama. Take your lists and use the intensity scale and the pendulum, as in Exercise 3. Break your list into categories as before. You will notice that you have very fixed patterns of emotional responses. The more intense your reactions are, the more predictable you are to other people. When your reactions to other people and events are predictable, it is easier for someone to manipulate you. To move into a reality where nothing is truly predictable and all is new, we must strive to leave our fear, anxiety and guilt behind. To function effectively in our own best interests, we must be free to respond to what is really happening, and to respond in a natural and spontaneous manner. All of our fears, anxieties, guilts and beliefs are related to past instructions or experiences; they are *never* related to the present moment. This is extremely important to realize. The present moment is new and has never existed before. Never drag old feelings or guilts into a new moment.

Consider carefully that the only thing you ever have in life is the present, the now. The past is old business; don't let it mess up the present, and never drag it into your future. From your present now, you command both your past and your future. In this chapter I discussed ways to reprogram negative beliefs from the past. In the next chapter, you will learn ways to program the future. Appreciate your now, enjoy it, unfettered by limiting beliefs, old fears, past experiences and future anxieties. Trust yourself, and you will trust life.

9

Out of Time

While discussing in the last chapter how our beliefs affect our reality, I asked you in Exercise 4 to write down your beliefs about time. In order to deal with past life recall and programming the future in this chapter, it is necessary to understand how time functions, and to separate our beliefs about time from what time really is.

In our culture, we believe that time is a fundamental law, something we have no control over. Time is the root assumption upon which we build the rest of our beliefs. Yet, time is only a convention agreed upon by human beings. Our concept of time is, after all, only an assumption, no matter how fundamental it seems to be.

Time appears to be fundamental because we use it to structure our lives; but time is only a measurement, like feet and inches. We invented time to help organize our lives. As with any measure, there is an agreement about what the standard should be, and then the measuring tools are calibrated to that standard. We tend to forget that the original agreement was arbitrary.

For example, none of us question the fact that a foot is twelve inches long. We accept it as one of the few consistencies in our lives. But why twelve inches? Why not eleven or fourteen? It is twelve inches because that was the original agreement. Time operates in much the same manner. There is an arbitrary decision about the divisions, and then an agreement of those divisions as standard. We come to believe that time is composed of minutes, hours and days, marching in linear fashion from the past, through the present, to the future. We have accepted the belief that time is something outside ourselves and beyond our control.

But that is only a *belief* we hold about time. Time is flexible. Think how long an hour is, when you are sitting in a boring lecture, and how short an hour is when you are having a good time. Dreams are a good example of the flexibility of time. In a dream, you can experience a day's worth of events in a few minutes. You can expand or contract time in dreams; you can also alter the sequence of time, mixing past, present and future all together.

Yet, in our waking reality, we insist on holding the belief that time is linear. This linear view of time—that is, the passage of time in sequence, yesterday, today and tomorrow—is a commonly held view because it fits so neatly into the belief that cause and effect is the primary relationship in the universe. We have all been brought up on the notion that the past is over and cannot be changed and that it conditions the present, which in turn conditions the future. Because we believe this, it is so. It is the cause and effect relationship in action. We believe that the past causes the present, so we make our reality reflect our belief.

There is another view of time. In this alternative view, events happen simultaneously, rather than sequentially. This idea is based on the assumption that time is a construction or belief system of human beings to structure their universe, and that it has no factual basis in reality. If the past exists simultaneously with the present and future, then all time periods can be experienced as easily as the present.

The past is found in our memories, and we can, by changing our focus, go back to any time we wish. The future is available through ESP, and that too is open to us through a change of focus. By knowing what *can* happen, we can take an active part in deciding what *will* happen. The ability to shift time periods is common among psychics, and it is this ability that enables them to predict your future and describe your past. This ability to shift the focus of time periods is available to us all. It requires a change in our beliefs about time, and some practice at shifting focus.

Past Life Recall

The possibility of past life recall became apparent to therapists when they tried to cause their patients to regress under hypnosis to an earlier time in their present life. While trying to uncover the childhood source of some adult fear, they hypnotized their patients and instructed them to return to a time when they were say, five years old. The patient would return to a time when he or she was five all right, but oftentimes when "five" in another century. For some time there was considerable confusion about what was happening, due to the therapists' limited beliefs about the structure of time. With enough documentation from many therapists, regression to a previous lifetime became an accepted tool in solving traumas in this lifetime.

What triggers the recall of a past life? It appears that recalling past lives is similar to recalling events in this life, the stronger the emotion surrounding that event or life, the easier it is to recall. As you review your life, you will notice that you have no particular memory of certain periods of time. There are other periods, though, that stand out clearly because of the strong emotions associated with the events. These periods are called "peak experiences." What triggers your memory of these things? Sometimes a piece of music from that time reminds you of the experience, and sometimes a particular scent. If you associate your grandmother with the smell of apple pie, then every time you are near that scent, you will think of her. If your relationship with her was a good one, you will probably love the smell of apple pie because it brings up the memories of the good times you and she had together. The smell of the pie will trigger your memory of the pleasant experiences associated with the smell of apple pie. If your relationship with her was unpleasant, then you will loathe the smell of apple pie, and try to avoid it. You will consciously block the memory of your grandmother. The ability to recall an experience or block an experience is a familiar phenomenon in this life. What may be unfamiliar is that this ability is used to block the unpleasant experiences of past lives as well.

Most blocking, of both present and past life experiences, comes from the attempt of the conscious mind to avoid pain. By blocking a painful experience rather than dealing with it, the conscious mind causes mystifying behavioral patterns. For instance, a person with a fear of water may have had a near-death experience in this life involving water. If the incident occurred in the near past, and the individual is aware of the event, then his or her emotional response to water is not a mystery. But, suppose the near-fatal drowning happened early in childhood or in another lifetime. Not remembering the incident, the person will puzzle over this "irrational" fear of water. The strong emotion remains, but the memory of the experience is blocked. To be free of the fear, the person has to go back to the event that caused it.

Going back to the event proves to be not so easy as it sounds. With hypnotism, however, regressing to an earlier time can be easily accomplished. Through the use of hypnosis, blocks to the subconscious mind are alleviated, and access to past lives is available. Having bypassed the blocks, the hypnotist will then suggest to the subject that he or she is a certain age, and will then move the subject backwards to the time when the trauma occurred. This process is called regression. An adult may achieve regression to age five, say, to find the origin of the problem, or may "jump" to another century to find the cause.

There have been countless times when psychiatrists have caused patients to regress to an earlier period, only to discover that the patient is recalling a life from another century.[6] This naturally happens when the cause of the problem lies within another lifetime. By recalling past lives we can get to the origin of many of our current problems. Relationships we have in this life are often continuations from other lives, just as our behavioral problems are. The more information we have about ourselves and others, the better able are we to deal with life's challenges and to grow.

Occasionally, in dealing with life's challenges, we experience a glimmer of our other lives. Spontaneous recall happens when a person responds to an emotional or physical situation in the present that triggers the memory of a similar situation from a past life. All of us have had the experience, at one time or another, of meeting someone for the first time and being sure we have met the person before. There is a sense of familiarity about the person that puts us at ease immediately. We go through the ritual of where we might have met, and when we can find no evidence of a former

---

[6]For more on past life regression, I recommend *Far Memory* by Denys Kelsey and Joan Grant, and *You Have Been Here Before*, by Dr. Edith Fiore. In both books therapists used cases from their practice in which problems in this life had their origins in previous lives. In the movie, *On a Clear Day You Can See Forever*, Barbra Streisand is hypnotized by her therapist and regresses to another century. The movie presents an interesting look at living many lives.

meeting, shrug off the familiar feeling as a mistake. In these cases, we have not gone back far enough. The feeling of knowing the person comes from another life. Our memory responds to the emotion, but has trouble placing the event. If our belief system allows for only one life, then we cannot allow the memory of another life to surface. If we are open to our past lives, then we can allow the memory of the past to surface, and we will remember where and when we knew the person. If we can have the feeling of having known someone before, then we are only a step away from remembering the time and place.

Although some people will choose to go to a professional to achieve regression, there are techniques that have been developed for the amateur. William Swygard,[7] a leader in the field, developed what he calls multi-level awareness, a way of being aware of the present and the past simultaneously. Marcia Moore[8] developed a similar technique which she calls "hypersentience." Both systems enable the amateur to take someone back through past lives. The first two exercises below present different techniques for past life recall. Try both techniques to see which one works best for you.

But first a word of caution. It is important to avoid using past life recall as a handy excuse for the problems you are facing today. Past life recall can give you information, but the information should be used to solve your problems, instead of a hook to hang the problems on. Although the cause of your problems may be found somewhere else, today's problems deserve today's attention.

Exercise 1 Past Life Recall With One Other: The subject should lie down on the floor or on a bed, and get comfortable; clothing should be loose, shoes removed. The setting is very important. The lights should be low so no glare distracts the subject. The person directing the recall, whom I will call the guide, should make sure all is ready for the session, then give the subject a light leg massage. Start just above the knees, one leg at a time, and massage lightly down the leg, briefly stopping at the knee to make sure

---

[7] I recommend *Awareness Techniques,* by Diane and William Swygard, a set of four booklets, to shed more light on the subject (see the Bibliography).

[8] *Hypersentience,* by Marcia Moore sets forth her method in a clear and easy-to-follow style (see the Bibliography).

it is relaxed. Continue massaging, bending the ankle when it is reached. Massage the feet and toes vigorously. After both legs are massaged, repeat quickly. Next, the guide should place the palm of his or her hand on the subject's forehead, and with just a little pressure, move the skin of the forehead up and down and sideways for a few seconds. Now everything is ready to take the subject back to another life.

As guide, begin by asking the subject to close his or her eyes. After a brief moment, ask the subject to become a few inches taller by stretching out through the bottom of the feet. Then say, "Tell me as soon as you have done this." When the subject says that he or she has accomplished this, say, "Go back to normal size. Tell me as soon as you have done this." Then, ask the subject to repeat the exercise, only the second time ask the subject to become "a foot" taller. "Tell me as soon as you have done this." When he or she does, pause again, then tell the subject to return to normal size. "Tell me as soon as you have done this." Repeat the foot-tall routine again. Each time ask the subject to tell you when he or she has accomplished the exercise.

Now, situate yourself behind the subject's head. "Become a few inches taller by extending yourself out through the top of your head. Tell me when you have done this." Then have the subject return to normal size. Instruct the subject to grow a foot taller through the top of the head. Repeat this exercise three times. The subject should tell you when he or she has completed each exercise.

Then continue with "Now, this time extend yourself through the head, face, body, arms, legs and feet. Blow yourself up just like a balloon. Tell me as soon as you have done this." Have the subject return to normal size. Throughout these exercises, be jovial and keep your voice firm and convincing. Be ready to laugh, and be sure the subject goes through these preliminaries quickly and smoothly. Once the subject has done the exercises well, there is no need to repeat them again.

Once again, ask the subject to blow up like a balloon, only much larger this time. When the subject reports that this is done, say: "Go quickly and stand in front of the building where you live; tell me when you are there." As soon as the subject reports being there, ask for a description of the scene: the door, door knob, windows, walkways, tree, shrubs, marks of any kind. When this description is done, say: "Go quickly and stand on the roof of the building and look down into the road; tell me when you are there." Ask for a description of any cars, trees and other objects that may be there. When this is done, ask the subject to go about five hundred feet up in the air and look down, and describe what can be seen from there. If the subject is in the one percent who protest at this, a quick reminder that his or her body is still safe in the room is enough reassurance; then repeat the request. To the objection that all this is just imagination, respond that this is an exercise in awareness, and continue.

After the subject has described to you things seen from this altitude, ask whether it is daytime or nighttime. When the subject tells you it is one or the other, ask why he or she thinks so. The subject will say something like, "It is daytime because everything is light and I can see just as if it were daylight, so it must be daytime." Or, "It is sort of twilight, you know, just after the sun has gone down." If the subject says it is nighttime or twilight, ask the subject to make it daytime, bright as sunlight. Again request that the subject inform you as soon as he or she has shifted focus. Then ask the subject to tell you why he or she thinks it is daytime. It is important to keep the dialogue going, keep the subject talking. If it was daytime to begin with, ask the subject to switch the vision to night. Turn the days into nights and back again at least three times, but be sure that you finish this phase with daytime, a very bright sunny day.

Then, ask quickly, "Who is making it night and day?" Most will quickly answer "I am!" If, however, the subject hesitates more than ten seconds, ask "Are you making it night and day?" He or she will agree. It is very important that the subject understand who is causing the change.

"Now, are you still high in the air?" The answer will be "Yes." Then say: "Please keep the scene very bright. Come back to earth in another lifetime that you lived many years ago. Come down quickly, as you go back in time. Bring your feet down quickly and firmly, but gently, and stand on the ground. Tell me as soon as you have accomplished this."

Watch the subject's face. As soon as there is eye movement under the lids, say: "Please look down at your feet and tell me what you are wearing on them." The subject is now experiencing a good vision of a previous life.

Remind the subject frequently to "Look out through your eyes and listen through your ears." Ask "What are you wearing on the lower part of your body?" Wait for the descriptions, but keep the person talking. Keep asking questions so that the subject describes what he or she *sees*, and does not make judgments. Insist that the subject do only what you say to do, and answer your questions. Remember to keep the questions in some semblance of chronological order. Move the person onward in time, skip a day, a week, a month or a year in his or her lifetime, to keep the subject moving and talking.

At the end of the lifetime, ask the person to go to an earlier lifetime, by requesting, "Come down in an earlier lifetime, look down at your feet and tell me what you are wearing on them."

At the end of the second or third lifetime, ask the subject to "die." Follow through the death, asking, "What happens next?" No matter what he or she reports, do not question the validity.

Before switching to another time period, or discontinuing the exercise, always ask the subject, "Do you see any need to continue at this time?" Let the subject decide when to stop.

Practice is essential. Soon an entire lifetime can be seen in a few minutes with all senses in focus. It is fun to be both the subject and the guide. Take turns, and do a lot of both. After three to five hours of "coaching" or assisting a person, the subject should be ready to explore his or her own past lives solo. The question technique is the hardest aspect of this exercise for most people to master. That is why it is important to be both subject and guide while you are learning this technique. Remember the question "What happens next?" This question can help advance the events of the lifetime. As soon as a subject can ask questions of himself or herself it is time to run through the exercise alone.

Exercise 2 Past Life Recall With One Other: The subject should lie down on the floor, a bed, or a sofa, with shoes off and clothing loose. He or she may want a covering blanket, because body temperature drops when one becomes relaxed. Soft lights and a peaceful setting are important. Before beginning, the guide should briefly describe the process to the subject, and suggest that the subject relax and be receptive.

The first step in the process is relaxation. The guide can suggest that each part of the body relax, as in the exercises in Chapter 2, or the guide can suggest resting in light, choosing color vibrations such as green or aqua, the most peaceful ones.

Next, have the subject repeat out loud the number one. After ten seconds, move the subject on to number two. Continue with the other numbers until you feel that the subject is sufficiently relaxed. Repeating the numbers provides a focal point for the subject's attention, and clears the subject's mind of extraneous thoughts.

When the subject's breathing has become deeper, his or her vibration level will have changed; now it is time to proceed to the next step. Ask the subject to climb a mountain, following a narrow, but clearly marked, path. Suggest, as the subject climbs, that he or she smell the scent of the trees, feel the sunshine on his or her face and body, and hear the birds. Tell the subject to come to a wide ledge on the mountain that looks out over a valley. There is a bench on this ledge where the subject can rest before going on. Then suggest that the subject is going on a trip to another time.

Now, suggest that the valley below appears to be filled with fog. Actually, the subject is now above the cloud line. As the subject looks over the clouds and fog, he or she will see the top of a rainbow. The ends are hidden in the clouds. Have the subject step onto the rainbow and slide down into the fog, all the way to the bottom. Ask the subject to describe what is there—what is on his or her feet, what is the clothing like, what are the surroundings like? Ask the subject where home is and what it is like; suggest that the subject go there and describe it to you. What is the subject's age and occupation? What year is it? Continue asking as many questions as you can think of to get as complete a picture as possible, and to keep the subject talking.

Now suggest that the subject move ahead five years and describe what happens then. Continue moving the subject ahead through the lifetime. If the subject gets into a situation that is highly emotional, like death, take the subject beyond the experience to a point just after the event, and then ask the subject to look back and describe what happened.

Be sure to ask whether or not any of the people in that lifetime are with the subject in this one, and, if so, ask the subject to identify who they are now. When you think that enough information about a particular life has been recalled, ask the subject to go through a nearby door and to climb the flight of stairs there, leaving that life behind. The flight of stairs is extraordinarily long. At the top of the stairs, there is a trap door opening out on the ledge where the bench is. Have the subject rest quietly on the bench before beginning the descent down the mountain. At the bottom, begin the backwards count of numbers, suggesting a return to the conscious state from which the subject started. Ask the subject to open his or her eyes when ready. Then talk about the experience.

This exercise can be done as frequently as the subject wishes. An hour at a time is usually enough. The most common mistake made is that the guide often moves along through the life too fast for the subject. Always inquire if there is any reason to remain at a particular point in time, before you move the subject ahead.

Exercise 3 Past Life Recall (Solo or With One Other): Having mastered the ability to recall past lives, you will, in this exercise, focus on a particular life. Begin as in the previous two exercises; relax, change your time focus and be receptive to your own memory. In this exercise, the difference is that you will select a specific past life experience to go to, rather than accept whatever past life memory your subconscious gives you.

Before you begin your relaxation, write down a specific problem from your present life. If you do not wish to choose a problem, then write down a question about a relationship in which you are involved, which you would like to understand better. Then, ask your subconscious if the cause of the problem, or the origin of the relationship, lies in a past life. Request, if this is so, that the particular part of your past life be shown to you that focuses on this issue. Then proceed as usual through one of the past life recall exercises (Exercise 1 or 2).

After the session, compare the information you got with the question asked. Did the information solve the problem? If not, perhaps you were not clear enough with your question. Be very specific about the information you want. This exercise can be done as often as you feel the need.

Programming The Future

What we do in our present will determine our future. The problem inherent in programming the future lies in getting the conscious and the subconscious into the same harness. As we have discussed before, the conscious self is the rational, thinking consciousness, and the subconscious self is where feelings reside. Our thinking and our feeling selves should be in harmony, but often they are at odds with one another. The conscious self dreams up the plans for the future and makes the decisions to put the plans into action. The feeling self is where the work is done to make those plans a reality. If the subconscious is in harmony with the plans, then it will work toward the materialization of the plans as designed by the conscious self. If the subconscious is not in agreement, it either refuses to do its part, or actively works against the conscious goal.

If programming your future does not work out as planned, then look to your subconscious for the stumbling blocks. Your belief system may need revamping. You may consciously desire to be wealthy, yet subconsciously believe that you don't deserve to be. It is only when there is complete harmony between your subconscious beliefs and your conscious desires that you will achieve results.

To create the future and have it happen, we must seed the subconscious or unconscious with the patterns and designs we want to appear. Our subconscious functions visually, rather than verbally. Symbols and images are its language. Therefore, when programming your future plans, visualize a desired future scene and place yourself in the scene. If you see a gorgeous office to work in, but forget to visualize yourself working there, then the message to your subconscious is incomplete. Make your designs and plans as complete as possible, and then remember to let go of them.

As was the case with your beliefs, if your new design conflicts with a previously implanted one, then the new one will not work. You must constantly adjust your design as new information becomes available. You must leave room in your program for insertions and changes.

The first step in programming the future is setting goals. The conscious setting of goals must be in harmony with your subconscious desires and beliefs. In the chapter on beliefs, you learned about the use of the word "should." If you are doing what you believe you should be doing, instead of what you really want to do, there will be a lack of cooperation between your two selves. If the contradiction between the "should" and the "want" is deep enough, the subconscious will intervene to prevent you from doing what you believe you "should" be doing. An accident or illness will provide a way out, and prevent you from performing the "should;" but what a price to pay! It is more effective to consult your inner self when making plans, and avoid inner conflict which leads to accidents and illnesses.

For example, I once made plans to take a trip, without consulting my inner self. Two days before leaving, I sprained my ankle. Aware that I had brought this accident on myself by thoughtlessly neglecting to cooperate with my subconscious self, I sat down with my pendulum to try and correct the oversight.

As I sat there with my crutches beside the chair, I realized that my inner self did not want to take the trip, but I was unable, even with the use of the pendulum, to find out why. Having committed myself to the trip, I then proceeded to ask my inner self to cooperate with me, by healing the ankle so that the trip could be made in greater comfort. I got an agreement. Within two days, the ankle had completely healed. Still, I wondered why my inner self was so reluctant to take the trip. After the trip, my conclusion was that my psychic side had perceived in advance how bored I would be on the trip, and had not wanted to go. I regretted going on the trip most of the time I was away from home. I had set an inappropriate goal and my inner self knew it.

We all strive to achieve goals.[9] It is natural to us, and we have the equipment to achieve any goal we set for ourselves—but only if the two sides of our nature are in agreement concerning the goal set. Our nervous systems, controlled by the subconscious mind, react to a desired goal by furnishing the energy to accomplish the goal. If the thinking side of the brain and the feeling side of the brain are in accord on one goal, it will surely be achieved. The inner self seems to need goals in order to be active. Lethargy and apathy are symptoms of a self that lacks goals. If there is nowhere to go, why get out of bed? Goals fire the inner self with enthusiasm, a life force that furnishes us with tremendous energy. We all need both short- and long-range goals. Working on a short-range goals will give us the confidence and patience to work on the long-range ones.

Exercise 1 Programming the Future - Goal Setting (Solo): The hardest part of programming the future is setting appropriate goals. This is an exercise to develop goal-setting skill. On a piece of paper, write down ten personal goals. Take each goal separately and ask yourself, "What will I gain from the achievement of this goal?" Then, "Why is this goal important to me?" If it turns out that the object of the goal is only to impress others,

---

[9]For more on goals, I recommend *Psycho-Cybernetics*, by Maxwell Maltz (see the Bibliography).

then the goal may not be achieved. A desire to impress others is an indication of low self-esteem, and you need to review your beliefs about yourself and make adjustments. After you have removed the inappropriate goals, separate the remaining ones into short- and long-range ones.

Exercise 2 Programming the Future - Goal Setting (Solo): Choose a short-term physical goal from your list. Make sure it is a reasonable one. If you are at your appropriate weight, and you make your goal losing five pounds in a month, it is highly unlikely you will succeed. The inner self knows what the right weight is and will thwart your attempts to go below it. Write the goal you have selected down on your paper. Ask yourself what the gain is from achieving this goal. Then ask yourself what action will be required to achieve this goal. For example, if you wish to get into good physical condition within a month, you will have to engage in some sort of physical activity. Think about and decide on the method best suited to your energy. If you hate to run, maybe bicycle riding would be more appealing to you. Once you have decided on the method, make a conscious commitment to achieve that goal. Do this exercise with one goal at a time until you get used to setting and achieving reasonable goals. Then and only then can you go on to more complex ones.

In the area of goal setting, it is important to note that you will get what you ask of yourself, so be careful. If your goal is to have a new car, you can achieve the goal, but you may have to take a second job to pay for it. If your goal is to have someone to love, make sure you include, "and who loves me." You get what you ask for, no more and no less.

Exercise 3 Programming the Future (Solo): Choose a short-term goal, something that can be achieved in a month, such as losing twenty pounds or generating four hundred dollars. Be reasonable. Write a complete description of what you wish to achieve. Be as detailed and as clear as you possibly can, because your goal will be in the form of pictures within your mind. Close your eyes and see the fulfillment of the goal as a photograph or a moving picture. As the picture becomes clearer, add more details to the writing. Work back and forth, writing and imaging in pictures, correcting, deleting and adding, until you have a picture that is as close to the desired goal as possible. Then release the image, secure in the knowledge that your goal will be achieved.

Exercise 4 Programming the Future (Solo): Having done the writing and image-making in Exercise 3, now visualize the achievement of your goal. What you desire is happening at the mental level already. As you visualize your goal actually coming true in the future, take note of your feelings. In order to have your goal realized you must seed your subconscious with the appropriate feelings in the present. Investigate the feelings; experience them. Positive feelings will give strength and energy to the achievement of your goal and negative feelings will destroy or warp the goal. The feelings that surface during your visualization process are a result of your beliefs concerning this goal. If the feelings are positive, you are on your way to successful achievement. If the feelings are negative, then it's "back to the drawing board" to correct those negative beliefs. Once you have straightened out your beliefs, your feelings will reflect the change. Then your goals will be easily achieved.

Exercise 5 Programming of the Future (Solo): This is an exercise I call "standing on the hypocrite's bridge." Imagine yourself standing half way across a bridge. On one side is an existing condition that you wish to change. On the other side is the situation as you would like it to be. Look at both sides clearly, but as dispassionately as you can. Next, begin to act as if the desired condition were here and now, even though you know the old condition still exists. Continue to act, "as if," and pretty soon the desired condition will actually be.

Once I set a goal of a new relationship with plants. The hypocrite bridge method worked well. I had never had a green thumb, and had little success at all growing house plants. Either I watered them too much and rotted the roots, or I neglected them and they died from lack of water. I had heard stories of people talking to their plants and getting responses. Then there were stories of experiments that involved praying over plants to heal them or make them flourish. These experiments sounded exciting and seemed to prove that some people were able to develop wonderful relationships with plants. All these ideas intrigued me. What I wanted was to make an experiment in which a plant flourished under my care and attention. I started by buying a small ivy plant, which I placed on my windowsill. It had three small leaves and was in good health the day I brought it home. Every morning I stood in front of this plant, speaking flattering words, which were not at all sincere. I was being a hypocrite, fully aware that I did not mean a word of what I was saying! I would say, "I love you, you are so beautiful," and similar phrases. Feeling foolish because I was so insincere, I found it difficult to go on. But I persisted. Daily I spoke to the little ivy plant. I was determined to change my relationship with plants.

Suddenly one day, as I stood there mouthing the same old phrases, I became aware that my feelings had indeed changed. My feelings now fit the words I used. How excited I became as real love for the little ivy plant flowed through me. The plant suddenly appeared truly beautiful to me. I realized that I had crossed the bridge. Now my goal had been achieved, by pretending the desired state was in effect all the time. It was important, though, that I be aware of my hypocrisy for if I suppressed my antagonistic feelings, I would only be kiddding myself.

One of the results of programming the future is that, once the program is set on motion, it will continue through its own momentum with little effort on your part. An example of how this works is shown in the following story. I needed a certain book to achieve one of my aims. All my efforts to acquire the book proved futile. Then one day, on impulse, I went into a bookstore that I passed on my way to do another errand. Wondering what I was doing there, I wandered down the aisles glancing at the books. Eureka! The book I had been looking for was on the shelf in front of me. Somehow, my inner self sensed the presence of the book there, and gave me the impulse to walk into the store and find it.

The impulse to complete unfinished business is part of consciousness itself. We find this urge exhibited by our ritualistic patterns. When the goal of sleep is to be achieved for a child, there is a good-night ritual. The child feels compelled to complete each detail of the established bedtime routine, before he or she can go to sleep. The familiar teddy bear must be clasped, the last drink of water drunk, the bedtime story completed, before the child drops off to sleep. Whatever ritual has been developed to achieve a certain goal, that ritual must be fulfilled before the goal is gained.

You can use this human inclination to achieve certain small, daily goals. Set up a pattern of behavior that culminates in success, and then faithfully follow the pattern until it is habit. Of course, these fixed patterns of behavior can make us rigid and inflexible, so be very careful in your selection of goals and rituals.

We create our future, in a personal sense, each moment. As we think and as we feel, we generate future happenings which will seem to come upon us from outside ourselves. The patterns of consciousness developed within serve as the stimulus to action. When those patterns are in someone else's design, however, we are controlled by that other person. We can change our future from what it would have been by examining what patterns exist, and by changing or eliminating them. We can create new and better patterns, giving ourselves a more satisfying life style.

10

Psychics, Mediums and Guides

In the last chapter you learned how to recall past lives and how to program your future. Although all of us can develop these skills, not everyone does. For one thing, it takes time to become proficient at a new skill. Some people are too impatient to wait until they have learned enough to program themselves. Others lack confidence in their ability to develop these skills. Such people seek others to do the programming for them. This chapter deals with those from whom such people seek help—psychics, mediums and guides.

Psychics

A psychic is a sensitive person who has developed his or her receptive skills enough to receive impressions from another person at will. The psychic achieves the no-mind state, allows the vibrations of another person to pass through, and describes what he or she feels or sees. A session in which this takes place is called a *reading,* because the psychic is, in fact, reading the other peson's vibration, or aura. The psychic receives impressions directly from the other person's subconscious, without interference or blocking from the conscious mind. People go to a psychic when the flow between their inner self and their outer self has been blocked, causing them to lose confidence in their ability to direct their own lives.

The danger in this approach is that some people build up a dependency on their psychic counselor and go regularly for advice. Some psychics encourage this. I used to give psychic readings, but stopped because I did not want the responsibility for others' lives. Dealing with my own life is challenge enough. Giving up doing readings meant that I had to find some other way to share my psychic knowledge, so I turned to teaching. Teaching enabled me to give people the tools to develop their own psychic skills so they could be independent, instead of relying on a psychic to make choices for them.

Although I encourage everyone to be their own psychic, some people are not ready. These people will seek counsel to deal with the issues of their life. Some will seek psychological help and some will seek psychic help. It is perfectly appropriate to seek help any time you need it, and from whoever you feel can provide it. It is important to remember that another person can only advise; you are the one who must make the decisions and then act.

A psychic can provide you with clarification and insight on the confusing issues of your life. Most of us are too close to our own problems to get perspective; so by finding someone less involved we gain an understanding of what is going on in our lives. The psychic "tunes in" to your present vibration and indicates what the probable future is if you continue on the course you have set. He or she can also tell you about the people around you, so you will have a better understanding of their behavior.

Usually, the information you get from the psychic is a confirmation of what you already know. If you are not in touch with your subconscious, it may be new to your conscious self. Remember, nothing the psychic says has to be. You have the power to change the future. What you are getting from a reading is information for you to use as you see fit. The only thing any counselor should give you is perspective. The responsibility for your life is your own, and so are the decisions you must make.

For some unknown reason, people seem to suspend their ability to evaluate information when it comes from psychics. They either accept all of what the psychic says, or they discount the entire reading. Seldom do they discriminate between accepting what resonates to their system and rejecting what does not. If a psychic gets one or two points right, the client is inclined to buy the whole package. It may be that those two points are the only valid ones. Psychics are like other people: they have good days and bad days. They relate easily to some people and less easily to others. They are not consistent. You must use your critical faculties. You must not believe everything that is said, only those things that are relevant at the time of the reading.

Besides being too gullible, clients of psychics tend to be too passive. If the psychic tells the person that something bad is going to happen, the client is likely to worry it into existence. We do, after all, attract what we fear. If the psychic tells the person that something good is going to happen, the tendency is to sit back and wait for it, instead of putting energy into making it happen. Either way, the client is not taking the responsibility for his or her own life. The client is letting someone else plant seeds in his or her subconscious, which the client then allows to grow.

Accepting the psychic's version of your life, without carefully screening the information, is just like accepting other people's beliefs and allowing them to control your life. In order to be successful at any psychic skill, you must be able to communicate with yourself. Good communication is necessary when analyzing other people's advice as well. If the psychic tells you something that does not resonate with your inner self, your subconscious knowledge of what you really are, then you should communicate this fact verbally to the psychic. Perhaps the psychic needs more information to assess what he or she is reading in you. Since the psychic deals largely with images, interpretation is through his or her own experiences. Communicate your own experiences so that the psychic can adapt the images to your life to give you a more meaningful reading.

Mediums

The level above a psychic is a medium. All mediums are psychic; not all psychics are mediums. A medium, unlike a psychic, can communicate with the spirits. There are two kinds of medium, a physical medium and a mental medium. The physical medium allows his or her body to be used by discarnates, persons on the spirit side of life. The mental medium simply relays messages from the spirits on the other side. Most of the mediums you are likely to meet are mental mediums, because physical mediumship is much harder to achieve.

Mediums have always been controversial, due to their claim that they can communicate with spirits. In centuries past, mediums were persecuted and ostracized. Because of this, they joined one another for support and formed their own communities. Two of these still exist today. One is Lilydale, New York, and the other is Cassadaga, Florida. These communities are made up almost exclusively of mediums. In these communities the mediums have message meetings, give readings and hold development classes, all available to the public.

Both physical and mental mediums hold seances. Seance is a French word which means a gathering of a group of people for the express purpose of communicating with people from the spirit side of life. A seance can be a quiet gathering, which differs very little from a Bible study group. Unfortunately, through the media and through charlatans, the seance has taken on a spooky, if not sinister, connotation. People think of seances as weird activities in which furniture moves and strange noises are heard. Seldom is this the case. Most seances are quiet affairs in which a group of people sit comfortably while the medium relates messages. Since the majority of mediums are mental ones, these quiet seances are the norm. Physical mediumship seances *can* include noises or tables moving, but they are seldom as weird as the movie producers would have us believe.

The effects of physical mediumship are more dramatic than those of mental mediumship, so, of course, charlatans have sought to duplicate the effects by mechanical means. As a result, they have eroded credibility of physical mediumship. Physical mediumship can take many forms, but the most dramatic is the materialization of loved ones. To do this, the medium sits in a darkened portion of the seance room, separated from the participants by a curtain or screen. This area is called the cabinet. The medium goes into a trance and allows the discarnates to borrow chemicals from his or her body to effect the materialization. The combination of these chemicals is called ectoplasm, and it can exude from any orifice of the medium's body.

Ectoplasm has been isolated and analyzed chemically. It is a combination of sodium, chlorine, oxygen, phosphorus, calcium, nitrogen, hydrogen and carbon. It can be gaseous, liquid or solid. Ectoplasm can be amorphous, having no shape, or polymorphous, taking many shapes. It has weight, whether it is visible or not, and can be photographed. (The National Spiritualist Church Association has more information on these matters.)

While the medium is in the cabinet, the discarnate borrows the ectoplasm and fashions it into a shape that will be recognizable to one of the participants of the seance. The seance is conducted in the dark so it is the phosphorus in the ectoplasm that provides a glow by which the people in the room can see the materialization. The reason for the dark room is that light dissipates ectoplasm. In fact, light deters the production of the substance. If light should suddenly appear during the seance, the ectoplasm will be withdrawm into the medium with such force as to seriously injure or even kill the medium. In most cases of materialization, the presence of the spirit is sufficient for the participant, so actual speaking is not necessarily a part of this kind of seance.

The trumpet seance can be almost as dramatic as a materialization. In the trumpet seance an aluminum horn, which usually comes in three sections and is collapsible, is used as a focal point for the spirit. Since discarnates have no voices, they must borrow ectoplasm from the medium to make a voice box or larynx through which to speak. The spirit speaker places the ectoplasm larynx into the trumpet and speaks. Sometimes the spirit speaks without the aid of the trumpet, although normally the voice is too soft to be heard so the trumpet is used for amplification. Once the spirit has control of the trumpet, the trumpet floats in mid-air, a rather spectacular effect. The voice can sound metallic or slightly distorted, the way our voice would if we were speaking through a megaphone. This kind of seance is also referred to as a direct voice seance, because the spirit speaks directly to the sitter rather than through the medium.

There is another phenomenon of physical mediumship called apportism. During a seance in which a medium is the key figure, apports, or objects having concrete solidity, can be brought into the seance room, or solid objects can disappear from the seance room.

This process is used by discarnates for many different reasons. The funniest case of apportism I ever encountered was when a visiting medium had replaced Reverend Burns at the church in Stamford while he went on a vacation.

The new medium's guide[10] informed us at one class that, if we would bring a bag of jelly beans to the next class, she would take all the colored ones, leaving the black jelly beans for her medium. But she asked us not to tell the medium, intending to surprise him. One of the students brought the bag of jelly beans, and it was placed on a small table in the center of the room. Sure enough, when the seance was over we found only the black ones left. Our visiting medium laughingly told us black was his favorite jelly bean!

In a more serious vein, apports are more often brought into the seance room for a specific reason. One evening, a crippled girl was given an old medallion, struck in the memory of Florence Nightingale. When it first arrived we heard the clunk as it materialized within the trumpet. A voice told us it was very hot, and when cool enough it would be placed in the crippled girl's lap. After it cooled, the trumpet floated across the room and dumped it in the girl's lap. An hour later, when the seance was over, we all crowded around to see it and feel it. The medallion was still remarkably warm, the heat seeming to come from within the object.

Another case I am familiar with concerns a man who attended a seance conducted by a spiritualist medium. A ring he had lost years ago in California was apported during the seance. It slid down the trumpet and fell into his hand. He said the ring was warm to the touch and that he was instructed to let it cool in his outstretched hand before investigating it, to allow for the original shape to solidify. Evidently, if he had handled the ring while it was still warm, he could have dented it or embedded his fingerprint in the ring.

A skeptic at heart, he nevertheless found the evidence overwhelming, since this ring had been especially designed and had been in his family for years. There were no known copies of the ring. He had not thought of it for years, and none of the participants of the seance had any knowledge of its existence.

Other physical phenomena can be demonstrated to show that there are laws governing the manipulation of energy and matter of which we are unaware. For this we should be grateful to mediums for the sacrifices they have made and the ridicule they have endured to make these demonstrations possible. They offer demonstrable evidence for our "doubting Thomas" minds.

To become one of these mediums is like becoming a concert soloist.

---

[10]Discarnate bodyguard. Read about guides on page reference.

First you need the talent, then the right instrument and finally a commitment to develop that talent to the exclusion of all else. At the end, the soloist at least gets praise, while all the medium is likely to get is ridicule. It is no wonder there are so few physical mediums. Fortunately, we still have mental mediums.

Once we accept the fact of the continuity of life, and the possibility of communication with the so-called dead, we no longer need physical demonstration, so a mental medium will serve us quite well. Such a person can be a liaison for us between the worlds of the seen and the unseen. A mental medium will have a conversation with a discarnate and then pass on what is said. It is like engaging a translator so that you can carry on a conversation with someone who doesn't speak your language. Since there is no physical demand placed on the mental medium, or on the discarnate, who has no physical form, the communication can be established easily and the contact maintained for a considerable period of time.

When you go to a medium to set up communications with a discarnate, you can choose to go alone, or with a group of other people. If you go alone, the session is called a reading. During the reading, you may talk with only one discarnate or with many, each taking a turn to give you messages from beyond. If you go with a group to the medium, the session is called a seance. Again, you may get messages from only one discarnate, or more than one, depending upon how many people are in the group waiting for messages from their loved ones.

In such a seance, the participants sit quietly in a circle or around a table. The medium may ask them to touch hands so that their energy is interconnected. They are asked to close their eyes, relax, empty their minds and be receptive to messages from the other side. Usually, the room is dark and quiet. The reason for this is that, as you raise your vibration to become more psychically sensitive, you automatically become more physically sensitive. Bright lights or loud noises become painful.

The medium adapts the room to minimize environmental interference. A medium may have a particular room set aside for seances, so that the vibratory rate in the room will be consistently peaceful, of high energy, and conducive to the seance. Most people feel the energy the minute they walk into the room, and if they are not familiar with the feeling, they may become a little uncomfortable.

During the course of the seance, the participants will receive messages from their loved ones. It is important to be skeptical. A really good medium will give an accurate description of the person, sometimes even the name and a message in the same kind of language pattern the person used when he or she was on this plane. Ask for details. If this really is someone you know well, there will be private jokes or nicknames which no one but you and the discarnate could possibly know. This is the kind of proof you require.

I know of a medium who was giving a message to a man, and she said: "Peanuts is here. I don't understand what that means. I wanted to say, Peanuts are here, but was told to say, Peanuts is here. I have no idea what that means. Can you place it?" "Yes," said the man, "Peanuts is my dog and he passed over some years ago. I've been hoping to hear from him." This is an example of a good medium. She had no way of knowing about the dog, she just communicated what she picked up. She did not try to interpret or edit the message. She gave it out and let the client deal with the information. To him, it was proof of the continuation of life.

Often the messages or details we get during a seance make no sense to us. There may be references to people we cannot place. Don't worry about it. Often, you will be able to place the person later, or you may have to check family history to see if such a person really is on your family tree. If you cannot place the information given, let it go. Don't worry about what you have received in the seance. Use what is helpful and disregard the rest. Keep a light-hearted attitude; regard the experience as an adventure.

The seance should be fun. Laughter raises your vibration and makes contact easier. Going to a seance should be like going to a party. It is, after all, a party with your spirit friends. Some of these friends are loved ones that you knew in this life, and some are from other times and lives, and some are spirit guides.

Guides

The area of guides is vague. One theory is that the guides are parts of our unconscious, to which we give form. Another theory is that these guides are separate entities assigned to us for our protection and growth. It really is a moot point what guides are, but it does not matter as long as we profit from the guidance they give.

Our needs determine the type of guides, or forces, as they are often called, we attract to ourselves. As we grow, our guides will change to reflect our new needs. Each guide is assigned to teach a particular lesson. When you are finished, that guide leaves and a new one comes. It is very much like school. When you master first grade you move on to second grade and a new teacher. Sometimes you will have several guides, just as you had several teachers when you got old enough for departmentalized education. Occasionally, you will have a family member as a guide for a period of time. This is especially true when you are going through a difficult time in your life and need support. They are available to you when you need them, just like family members on this side of life. You can pick up a phone and call a family member when you feel like it. You have the same access to family members on the spirit side of life. They may be busy with their own activities, but can always break away for a visit to give us guidance.

Most guides won't interfere with our lives unless we are on a course of self-destruction. They are there for us, but we must decide to ask for their help and guidance. If we choose not to accept it, there is little they can do. After all, we do have free will. We can totally block guides. People who have trouble accepting help from people on this plane are likely to have trouble with people from the other planes. You have to want help to get it. Also, you must ask for it. If you want help from a spirit guide, but are not in contact with one, you can go to a medium, who will introduce you to a guide, or act as an intermediary between you and your guides. If you want to meet your guides, but do not wish to go to a medium to be introduced, here is an exercise you can do by yourself.

Exercise 1 Meeting Your Guide (Solo): Do your relaxation exercises, and drift into your centered, no-mind state. Choose a natural setting that is special and private in which to visualize yourself. It may be a real place to which you have been, or an imaginary one. If you are a person who enjoys the woods, visualize yourself walking through a forest. Feel the softness of the pine needles under your feet, smell the rich earth and the pine trees. See the sun streaming through the trees, and listen to the birds. As you walk along, notice the brook to your right. It sings as the water skips over the stones, and the water is fresh and clear, sparkling as it catches the sunlight. Walk along until you come to a clearing by the brook. Grass and moss grow on the banks of the brook; it is very peaceful there. Sit down and rest. Drink in the peace of the forest. Then, look in the direction from which the brook flows. Way off, in the distance, see a tiny dot of blue light. The light seems to be suspended above the brook, just glowing. As you watch it, the light begins to move down stream, coming toward you. As the light moves toward you, it gets bigger and more luminous. As the luminous mass gets closer, it begins to take the shape of a person. Finally, the shape is close enough for you to see who it is. Invite him or her to sit down next to you. Notice how comfortable you feel with this being. Ask what he or she is called, if you do not know the person. Talk about your problems and ask for any advice you want. After you have had a long enough conversation, ask your friend or guide to meet you there on another occasion. Slowly leave the clearing and the forest and come back from your meditation. Rest secure in the knowledge that you can go back there anytime you choose. If you are unsuccessful with this exercise, it may mean that you are not ready to meet your guide, or that you are afraid. Do not push. When the circumstances are right, it will happen.

Exercise 2 Meeting Your Guide (Group): This exercise is similar to the preceding one, only this time you lead a group. Do the relaxation exercises and breathing until everyone is sitting comfortably in a meditative state with their eyes closed. Suggest that each one is alone on a beach by the ocean. Suggest that the rhythm of the ocean is relaxing and peaceful. Let the water wash away whatever problems and negativity they may have.

When I do this exercise, I use a recording of the sound of surf for effect. It helps make the experience more powerful. I set the record before we start, without telling anyone. I sit by the record player, and, when I get to the sound of the ocean, I quietly move the needle onto the record, which is already spinning, and turn the volume up slowly, so they won't hear any clicks and be distracted from the exercise. Once they actually hear the sound of the ocean, they can visualize being there more easily.

After they have been enjoying the peace of the beach for a while, suggest that they turn their heads to the left and see a dot of blue light, way up the beach. Suggest that the dot of light starts moving toward them, getting larger and more luminous, the closer it gets. As the light gets closer, it begins to take human form, until they can identify the person. If the person is unknown, suggest that the participant ask the guide his or her name. Suggest that the guide be invited to share your blanket, and enjoy the beach with you. Have a pleasant conversation, and suggest that you might meet again on a different day. Tell the group that it is time to say goodbye to the guides and leave the beach.

During this part, I turn the volume of the record player down, slowly, so, as the sound is reduced, they get the feeling of actually walking away from the beach. Tell them to come back to the room you started from, and when they are back, to let you know by opening their eyes. Allow each one to return at his or her own pace. Do not talk until the last person has opened his or her eyes.

The number of variations on these exercises is limited only by your imagination. If you have a fireplace and it is winter, make up a cabin-in-the-mountains fantasy. Use what is available in your environment. The visual aids and sound effects will strengthen the experience.

As we come to the end of this chapter on psychics, mediums and guides, remember that these are tools available for enlightenment. They should not be used to impress others.

Keep the following anecdote in mind, whenever you feel the urge to show off your psychic skills:

There was a man who practiced walking on top of the water until he was able to demonstrate it to others. Proudly he showed off his skill to a master teacher. "Look at me!" he cried, "I can walk on water." The master made no answer. "Don't you think that is wonderful?" he cried. "Perhaps," replied the master, "but it is so much easier to pay a few cents and be rowed across."

11

Psychic Skills At Work

I purposely ended the last chapter with the anecdote about the man who walked across the water to impress the master, to point up why our psychic ability appears to vacillate. Sometimes we have access to it, and at other times we do not. From observation, it appears that emotional needs that can be fulfilled by no other means are what give us access to our psychic skills.

The man who walked across the water had an emotional need to impress the master. But the master's reply was a subtle reminder that the man had misused his skill. Since it was possible to be rowed, it is probable that the man would fail at a second attempt to walk across the water. The original need, to impress both himself and the master, was fulfilled by the original feat, and the inner self would feel no compulsion to perform the feat a second time, when there was no real need.

Need seems to provide the access to the psychic skills. Need provides the access to *all* levels of our consciousness—logical, psychic, subconscious, dreaming, and so on. Our different levels or streams of consciousness function within laws of the universe which we know little of; but which level of consciousness functions, and when, appears to have a direct correlation to need. If the need we have is best fulfilled by our logical consciousness, then we will feel a compulsion to use logic to alleviate the need. If psychic consciousness will best fulfill the need, then that is the consciousness we will use. Need provides the compulsion. There appears to be a great inner force that works toward fulfilling our needs. Our inner self will attract what we must have to fulfill the need, and use the consciousness that is best suited to the task.

It has been my personal experience that psychic consciousness operates most efficiently in areas of great emotional need. The most common experience of this, well-documented during two world wars, is telepathic communication between mothers, away from the battle, and sons, in a war zone. Here, the emotional need of the mother to know about her son's well-being is intense. The son's need to reassure his mother of his safety is strong, yet no fast method of communication is accessible. In order to alleviate the tension between need and fulfillment, a strong telepathic bond is built between the mother and son, almost unconsciously. The mother will go about her business at home, "knowing" that her son is still all right. If you ask her how she knows, she would respond that she just has a "feeling." Yet, the instant her son is wounded, she would "know" that also. Often, at the time of injury or death, mothers "hear" their sons calling to them, yet the son is on the other side of the world.

While living together, the mother and son may never have developed any telepathic rapport, because other means of communication were available to them. When separated, and the son placed in a perilous situation, the need and desire to communicate between the mother and son is so intense, with no other means available to alleviate the tension, that a telepathic bond develops between the two.

This is a perfect example of emotional needs being solved by psychic abilities, because there was no other resolution. Had a phone been available the resolution of the emotional need probably would have been by direct voice contact over the phone.

What happens to our psychic abilities, though, when the emotional need of one person is at odds with the emotional need of another? I will relate a personal experience and you can see for yourself what happens.

As a member of a weekly mind-to-mind healing group, we were given a case to work on one winter evening. The case we were given was the father of a friend of mine. He was in the hospital, having just undergone surgery. Naturally, my emotional need was a desire for him to be well, both for his own sake, as well as for my friend's.

Using my usual technique, I constructed a scene of my friend's father in a hospital bed with tubes connecting him to life support systems. My imagery was excellent. I was focusing my attention on the scene I had constructed, when I saw something suddenly pop into the scene, which I had not designed. It was a hooded figure, standing on the other side of my friend's father's bed, shaking his head in a negative manner. I caught the thought, "Leave him alone." Being stubborn and persistent, I ignored this intruder and continued on with my psychic efforts and the healing procedure.

I was more intent on accomplishing what I had set out to do than with considering the effects of my psychic efforts on my friend's father and his own needs concerning his illness. Blind to the fact that his needs were at odds with my own, I pushed on with the healing exercise.

Suddenly, in my mental scene, I found a tremendous distance between myself and the man in the bed. He was far below me, a minute image, and I was high up in the sky somewhere. I heard voices singing; a "Requiem" came to my mind. But the voices were joyous, thousands of them; the harmony was glorious. I listened and wondered what was happening. Then looking down again at the man in the bed far below me, I suddenly was at his side. The hooded figure was still in the scene and seemed to laugh. Frustrated by not understanding what was going on, I stubbornly tried to send more healing energy to the man. As quickly as before, I was high up in the sky, while he remained in the bed far below. The chorus sang louder than ever! This new experience was too much for me, and I was a bit shaken by it. I let go of my mental healing scene, and opened my eyes and waited for the rest of the group to finish their efforts. I was puzzled by the incident and my lack of success at sending my friend's father any healing energy.

The mystery was cleared up a few days later, and my experience at the group meeting finally made sense to me. My friend's father was dying, and it was right and proper that he should leave the physical plane at this time. I was interfering by trying to send him healing energy he did not want, hence my attempts were blocked.

I was, however, delighted to hear from my friend, his daughter, that, a few days before he died, he informed her that all the nurses were numbskulls, for they did not believe him when he told them he had heard angels singing! He said it was beautiful music, and he had become aware that he was dying. His sense of peace and harmony made his death a more joyful occasion both for him and for his daughter.

Apparently, the hooded figure in my mental image was trying to tell me, by shaking his head no, that I was misusing my ability, because my friend's father did not need the healing energy. When I refused to take notice of his message, he tried to jolt me with the singing, yet still I refused to learn, so my attempt was frustrated.

The first two examples I have used were highly charged emotional situations. However, even when the need is less intense, our psychic skills function just as well if no other means of resolving the need is available. The following illustration is an excellent example of psychic abilities used every day.

Katherine Edson Mershon, the author of three books on Bali, went to the island in 1931 and remained there until 1941. She found that ESP was a commmon way of communicating among the Balinese. Lacking phones, ESP seemed a natural way to communicate with one another when separated by distances. They called it "news on the wind," when they picked up telepathic messages. Mrs. Mershon related the following experience in one of her books: "Being among people who use ESP so often was a very strange experience at first. People would say to me, 'Oh, we knew you were coming,' and I'd ask, 'Who told you?' They'd just shrug as though I'd asked a ridiculous question."

In time, Mrs. Mershon said that she too became proficient in the use of ESP. She recalled using her skill to communicate with a Balinese fisherman named Yoman. When tourists wanted to go out to the coral reefs, she would just think, "Yoman, come in. Yoman, come in" intently. His arrival would depend on how far out to sea he was when she called. If he was close to shore, he came in immediately.

The telepathic ability seems to function on a daily basis in primitive societies, where so-called modern conveniences are unavailable and preconceived ideas about the existence of ESP are positive rather than negative. Actor Peter Finch once related the story of how, shortly after World War II, a friend of his on the faculty of Sydney University arranged to take him along on an expedition to study a tribe of Australian aborigines, some of the most primitive people on earth. One day, when Finch was about 500 miles from the ocean and far from any other body of water, everyone was talking excitedly about a boat. He couldn't get any definite explanation; they just repeated again and again that somebody in a canoe was in trouble. Finch made a note of it in his diary and then forgot it. When he returned to the coast, he showed his notes to a missionary who was astonished at the notation about the boat and the date. "On that day I sent a boy from that tribe on an errand by boat;" the missionary told Finch, "he turned over in the surf and nearly drowned." Finch was amazed at the pron unced demonstration of ESP in humans.

He had had a previous experience of psychic ability, but with an animal. During the Second World War, he was manning an anti-aircraft gun in Australia. "An hour before we got warnings from lookouts, we'd know Japanese planes were coming because our dog would behave strangely," he said. "He couldn't have heard anything. It was a sixth sense that told him."

Finch isn't the only person to have experienced ESP in animals. In the book, *Kinship with All Life*, by J. Allen Boone (see the Bibliography), we read of a dog with pronounced ESP skills. Boone tells how disadvantaged he felt when he realized that the dog could read his mind, while he could not tell what the dog was feeling or thinking. There are many stories in the book that will appeal to animal lovers and encourage readers to develop their own ESP, in order to better communicate with other species.

Anthropologists claim that ESP is prevalent in animals and among primitive people, while in more civilized societies it has become stunted so that it only works occasionally. In our society, it seems to work best when a real tragedy is involved; an intense emotional experience.

Consider the following account. In June, 1974, in Idaho, two men, strangers to one another living some 300 miles apart, used their clairvoyant abilities to pinpoint the exact spot where the body of-a missing boy lay.

Gerald Sturn, a twenty-five-year-old plumber, decided to see if he could help find the boy with psychic skill. Before closing his eyes in preparation for sleep, he focussed his attention on the missing child. As he was focussing, a scene he did not recognize floated across his mind. He could see a mountain split in two, with rocks and boulders lying at the base. He felt sure that this was where the boy was. His intense desire to find the boy led him off early the next morning to the search area. An eleven-year-old boy, named Jeff Hodgson, who had lived in Pocatello, Idaho, was missing. More than a week before Sturm's clairvoyant vision, Jeff had become separated from a team of youngsters on a survival course. For ten days, hundreds of searchers scoured the wasteland, under a scorching sun, hunting for Jeff. At times, the searchers passed within a few feet of the boy's body, but did not see him, because of the rocks.

Sturm did not tell any of the other searchers about his clairvoyant vision when he arrived at the search area, a place called Split Butte. The searchers headed east, because the southern area had been thoroughly covered. Sturm headed south. He sensed he was right in his choice of direction, because when he had reached Split Butte, he felt as though he was stepping into his vision of the previous evening. He located the rock in his vision, and then he saw Jeff's hat, then his shoes and socks. He found the boy's body behind a ten-foot-high rock. Temperatures had been over 110 degrees during the week, and the pathologists, after doing an autopsy, believed the boy died of heat exposure.

Elbert Glehn, a seventy-one-year-old retiree, living in Boise, Idaho, had a spontaneous vision of the area where the boy's body lay. The vision was so clear and so intense, Glenn could not shake it. Twice he had the vision, and the intensity of the vision finally made him phone a local newspaper, "The Idaho Statesman." The paper printed an account of Glenn's clairvoyant vision. The description that Glenn had given the newspaper was incredibly like Sturm's vision. Both visions duplicated the spot where the body was found by Sturm.

Both men knew of the missing boy, and both had an intense desire to aid the searchers. Time was of the essence in finding young Jeff, due to the extreme heat. In both men, desire to help another human being triggered visions beyond their normal, everyday perceptions. In this case, clairvoyance was the psychic faculty best suited to resolving the tension between the need to help the boy and the fulfillment of the need.

It seems that in our very "civilized" culture some of our mental faculties have atrophied, so that they function only in times of great emotional stress. Our more primitive neighbors seem to have retained their psychic faculties and to use them in their everyday lives in much the same manner they would use logical reasoning. The appropriateness of the situation determines which faculty they will use.

The closest we come in our culture to this kind of appropriate use of all our faculties, both logical and psychic, is in the area of dowsing. Dowsing is predicated on the need for some element, usually water, buried beneath the earth's surface. A dowser simply walks across the land, holding out a rod. When the dowser nears the place where the element is buried in the earth, the rod will vibrate. Although water is the normal target, dowsers can also locate deposits of oil, salt and minerals.

Dowsing has existed for centuries, and historic accounts of "water witches" relate tales of individuals who developed the skill of finding water for farmers who needed the water for their animals and households. Certainly the psychic ability of dowsing was the appropriate faculty to use in finding water, especially since our present-day electronic gadgetry was unknown.

Due to its long history and the great success of its practitioners, dowsing is one of the few psychic skills that is practiced consistently in our culture. Dowsing has become so popular and useful that individual practitioners have banded together in groups all over the world. Nearly every country has its association of dowsers. In the United States, the American Society of Dowsers has its headquarters in Danville, Vermont. Every year they hold an annual convention so that people interested in dowsing can share their ideas and techniques. Training is given the novice dowser at every convention.

Because dowsing is so prevalent, a lot of research is done on this psychic skill. A very interesting piece of research was done with dowsers in Britain. The researchers gathered together a group of dowsers that had the highest success rate. These people had been very successful in finding water for farmers and property owners who needed a source of supply. Yet, when tested by doubting scientists in circumstances where there was no real need, the entire group failed. It seemed as though their own subconscious balked and refused to perform when the "need" was inappropriate.

When we can successfully learn to integrate all our streams of consciousness, then instances of psychic ability will be far more prevalent in our own society. We will then not need extreme emotional situations to get at our psychic faculties for they will have become a normal part of our daily living. Our psychic abilities will no longer vacillate, but will be available to us when appropriate.

12

Psychic Development

Many people have spontaneous psychic experiences unexpectedly at one time or another. Sometimes, if the person is unprepared and does not know how to interpret it correctly, the spontaneous development of psychic sensitivity can be distressing. Indeed, as you practice techniques to develop your psychic skills and arouse the dormant aspects of your consciousness, you are likely to have some unfamiliar experiences. The purpose of this chapter is to help you be prepared, not only so that you can appreciate and enjoy your new perceptions, but so that you can reassure and counsel others when their psychic faculties open up unexpectedly.

Often such people go to psychiatrists, priests or ministers. With very few exceptions, such "authorities" have no training in psychic-development counseling. Depending on the extent and character of the "symptoms," a person may be treated for anything from eczema to psychosis by well-meaning but uninformed helping professionals.

What are some of the "symptoms" of psychic faculties opening up? Physical sensations around the head area are quite common, such as a tingling of the scalp, a tickling sensation on the face, or a feeling of pressure around the top of the head, as if a band were being tightened. These physical sensations usually emanate from those portions of the brain which are aroused to new levels of consciousness. As your brain becomes accustomed to the new states of consciousness the physical sensations will cease, much as, when a new shoe finally gets broken in fully and fits your foot easily, you no longer notice either shoe or foot.

As your visual psychic faculties develop you may begin to perceive psychic energy as tiny sparks of light. At first visible only in darkness or dim light, like miniature fireflies darting to and fro in random patterns, they may eventually be visible even in direct sunlight if you look for them. You may find yourself seeing auras around people, animals, plants, even "inanimate" objects under certain conditions. You may choose to look at them or not, just as you choose whether to look at the reflection in a store window or the objects behind the window. You are in control at all times, because you determine where your attention is placed.

Everyone has all sorts of chatter going on inside. This is what the novelists call "internal monologue," though often there is more than one voice in conversation. If you hear voices and want to turn them off, use the same technique that you use every day when you want to listen to just one person in a crowded room, or when you want to study undisturbed by ticking clocks, street noises, television sounds or conversations. You don't have to "will" them to disappear, just focus your attention on something else that is more interesting to you. Everything thrives on attention; by withdrawing your attention and focusing it elsewhere, you take away the energy that keeps unwanted inner voices active. It doesn't matter whether a person is in the body or disembodied, when you stop paying attention eventually they stop talking.

Your natural empathy with the pain or physical discomfort of others may become amplified. You may inadvertently take the sensations into your own body. As you develop your psychic skills you should be on the watch for this phenomenon, especially if you are naturally empathic. The way to handle this is to question your own body about whose pain or discomfort it is. Simply ask: "Is this pain mine or someone else's?" Be clear in your desire to know. If you learn whose pain it is, you may want to do some psychic healing with the person; the link of empathy that has manifested can be used as a channel for healing. If you get no information in answer to your question, order the pain to leave your body immediately if it originates in another. If it does not leave, you must claim it for yourself and deal with it to find out what your body is telling you.

With your increased sensitivity you may notice that you pick up other people's emotional states, such as depression or anger. When you feel a strong emotion or a change of emotional state, ask yourself "Is this feeling mine or someone else's?" Feelings are contagious only if you allow them to be. Sit down, relax and close your eyes. Ask to see the image of the person from whom you picked up the feeling. If nothing appears, ask yourself the cause of the feeling. Don't think about it, just ask and wait for an answer: it is too easy to rationalize feelings, to pick something that bothers you and use it to justify feelings that really are out of proportion for that target. Finally, if you come to no clear conclusion of the matter, end the session with the command "If this (depression, anger or other feeling) originates in another, let it depart immediately from me!"

Everyone always has mental imagery, but not everyone is aware enough of mental images to distinguish them clearly from what their eyes see. This is the basis for illusions and hallucinations of all sorts—and, incidentally, the basis for a great deal of confusion and misunderstanding between people when they relate to their images of one another instead of reality. With your increased awareness of your own inner states and your growing psychic sensitivity, you may experience images arising into awareness that are undesirable to you. Deal with these just as you do with voices: turn your attention to something that interests you more. Either look at objects or pictures that are pleasing and interesting to you, or call up the images of places, people or things of which you have fond memories. You can also turn images away by giving a clear order to your subconscious that you refuse to give them room or attention, and that in the future your subconscious is to repel them with vigor. Or you can order the images to enter your awareness from the left, keep moving toward the right and leave on the right side. Keep the images flowing until they cease; watch them without involvement, patiently waiting for them to fade because of your disinterest.

If ever you feel the invisible presence of something which is repugnant to you, face it squarely. Even if you think it may be your imagination, treat it as if it were real and command it to leave your space. Speak firmly, with your attention focussed intensely on the space which you feel it is occupying. Continue with steady regard and firm intension until you feel that the presence is gone. If you wish, call on higher beings to assist both you and the unwanted presence. Remember that free will is a basic law of the universe; remind the presence that it may not intrude on your space and your awareness without your permission. If you feel more charitable you may want to ask what it wants; in any case, you may ask higher beings to give it what it needs.

Sometimes people who are of a nervous temperament overstimulate their nervous systems in their enthusiasm to progress with their psychic development exercises. Even if you are not high-strung, you may feel yourself becoming nervous, uncomfortably excited and tense. You can use color to slow and cool your consciousness if it gets overstimulated.

Exercise 1 Breathing Color (Group or Solo): First, work with your breathing and your favorite relaxation exercise to slow down and relax your physical body. Then, with your eyes closed, imagine a pale green cloud, cool and healing, about ten feet in front of you: bluish green, pale and translucent. As you continue to breathe slowly and deeply, completely relaxed and comfortable, watch it move closer with each breath; watch it come to hover over your head and then descend to envelope your body from head to foot. Then sense the cloud with every breath entering into your body and spreading through it. Take three deep, relaxing breaths to complete this process.

If you feel a need to continue to a deeper level of relaxation and healing, repeat the process with a second cloud of pale blue, with the quality of a freshly washed clear blue sky and a cooling breeze. On an even deeper level after that, repeat the process a third time with indigo, the deep, translucent color of the night sky that gives us rest, the color of the "divine Mother" who loves us all with a profound and unconditional maternal love. Feel that love caressing you as you breathe in the color indigo, a deep blue-violet verging on black.

The context within which you do your exercises to develop your psychic skills is very important. It should be the kind of environment that is helpful and supportive to you, with colors and furnishings that please you; you should feel good about it. It should be self-contained: you should be sure of your privacy; all the materials you need should be prepared in advance; and the time for your practice should be protected from interruption and from the distraction of other commitments.

Before beginning a session, spend a few minutes relaxing and allowing thoughts and images to arise into your awareness from your subconscious; jot down any reminders and tell you inner self that you will take care of this unfinished business later. (You have to *really* attend to it later, or you run the risk of not being believed when you talk to your inner self—something you definitely want to avoid!) Then use your favorite procedure for psychic protection, such as surrounding yourself and your exercise space with white light. Some additional protection procedures will be given further on in this chapter.

Working with a group of friends who share your interest in developing your psychic skills can be beneficial. It is more fun when it is shared, and enthusiasm is a key to success. Choose your group carefully to be compatible with one another and with yourself. Each member should be in good health, mentally and physically, not high-strung or preoccupied with the spookiness or glamor of psychic powers. Encourage the group to keep cool, stay serene, and above all to cultivate a sense of humor. A deadly serious approach is just that—deadly. Keep it light, keep it fun and each person will be freed to develop and grow in the way that is most appropriate and beneficial.

As you continue to meet and practice together, your group empathy will increase. This will speed your progress. If you find a member seems to hold the group back by lack of interest, excessive talking of things outside the subject chosen for the session or other disruptive behavior, find a kind way to eliminate that person from the group. The shared world-view of the group should include the belief that it is possible to increase one's awareness, and that exploring the unknown is desirable. The group members should feel eagerness to train themselves to use their psychic skills in a positive way; people who hope to use psychic skills to harm or control others should be immediately weeded out, for the boomerang effect of their actions may come back on the group as well as on the individuals directly responsible. Adopt the ancient coven ethic, "An ye harm none, do what ye will."

As your group empathy increases, your power to attract or repel energies increases also. Use this increased strength in your exercises, beginning with your protection procedures at the start of each session.

Here is the general outline of a procedure which your group can adapt to its particular circumstances and needs. Create an affirmation that the group can speak in unison; make sure that the meaning is clear and that, while speaking it, the meaning is held in awareness by each member of the group. Formulate the affirmation to embody the feelings the group would like to be surrounded with, in their protective field. Create an image that embodies those feelings, a picture to hold in the mind while speaking the affirmation.

An example of such an affirmation is: "The great white light of truth surrounds us now, protecting us from all harm. I will that this power remain with us and assist us to apprehend truth in all that we do. Only good can enter this field of white light, the great white light of truth. So be it." (Substitute "me" for "us" to use this by yourself.)

Other examples of such affirmations are the "Great Invocation" printed at the beginning of many of the Alice Bailey books, and "The Pattern on the Trestleboard" in Paul F. Case's *The Tarot, Key to the Wisdom of the Ages* (MaCoy Publishers). For those with strong religious beliefs, the singing of favorite hymns will energize the atmosphere and set a proper tone for either a group or individual session.

Good visualizations generally have to do with surrounding your space with a field of energy having a definite boundary. You may visualize the line of demarcation, the interface between you and the world, as a skin or membrane that can resist penetration or allow it.

Exercise 2 Aura Shield (Solo): Close your eyes and visualize a membrane about two feet from your body on all sides, like the tough translucent membrane around the liquid contents within an eggshell, but much finer, so subtle that it moves with every vibration, every puff of a breeze. See this skin as tough and healthy, with a fine texture and no holes or weak spots; if you find any, heal them with your imagination.

To strengthen this protective field, you might imagine a large paint brush sweeping a nice feathery border all around it in a beautiful color; or beam an imaginary flashlight all around the edges, emitting strength and clarity. Use images that tickle your fancy, any symbol that carries the message of a strengthened aura, a resistant interface.

You might want to make the membrane selective as to what it lets in and out. Once, when I wanted to keep out the emanations of fear from a crowd when the university campus was in turmoil and lots of upsetting events were taking place, I surrounded myself with the egg-membrane after I had picked up the negative feelings. Unwittingly, I had sealed them in with me! After a moment of intense nausea and dizziness I realized what must have happened and imagined a broom sweeping dust, dirt and bad stuff out of my aura. In this case I would have done better to be more selective when I set up the psychic shield, but because I acted out of fear I acted hastily.

Another good image is a coccoon, the shroud of silk that insect larvae spin around themselves for protection while they are transformed into butterflies. This protective quality is the reason why silk is often recommended for wrapping tarot cards, crystal balls and the like. You can visualize yourself (or your group) surrounded by strands of silvery-white light, like silken threads.

Everyone has access to the unlimited energy of the entire universe. Of course, no one person uses very much energy at any one time, but an infinite supply is there at need. Sometimes people cut themselves off from their energy supply, because of negative feelings about themselves and the world. Usually this results in various forms of illness; sometimes these people become known as "psychic leeches." When they draw on your energy reserves unconsciously, you begin to feel tired, sometimes sleepy. You should realize that these people are stuck in a psychic posture that is unhealthy for them and for those around them. If you are sympathetic to their need, you have the ability to draw on the universal supply and send them the excess you don't need for yourself, with the following exercises:

Exercise 3 Boundless Energy (Group or Solo): Relax, close your eyes and imagine yourself immersed in an immense ocean of energy. Even though you can't imagine any limit or boundary to this ocean, realize that is just a drop from the universal supply: there is no possibility of running out. Feel this energy flowing into you, through you, and out of you, like a river. As you breathe in, it flows in through the top of your head, your feet and your chest; as you breathe out, it flows out through your arms and hands and out of your chest from your heart. Pause before exhaling each time, and imagine a storage tank within you being filled; when it overflows, mentally direct the energy to the person who needs extra energy. Visualize the person immersed in this same ocean of energy, taking it in with each breath and filling an inner storage tank. When you are done, make sure you use up any excess energy with psychic or physical exercise, to avoid the discomfort of psychic indigestion!

Exercise 4 Energy Cloud (Group or Solo): Relax, close your eyes and imagine yourself under a cloud of white light, like brilliant sunlight. The cloud is oval, about six feet from top to bottom. Take as much time as you need to get this clearly focussed in your awareness. Allow all intruding thoughts and images to pass through your awareness until they cease to come, then take a deep breath and hold it to a slow count of twelve. As you slowly exhale, experience the white cloud descending upon you and enveloping your entire body. You will feel a tingling sensation, usually starting with the feet and hands, spreading upward and inward throughout your body and finally including your head. This is the subtle psychic energy the yogis call *prana*, which is necessary to your physical, emotional and psychic well-being.

Sit quietly for three or four minutes until the tingling sensation wears away, then repeat the process. After the second time, rest about five minutes, and do it again. End with a five minute rest period.

The more you do this, the easier it becomes and the less time it takes. You may even become able to re-energize yourself when you have a few minutes of time, sitting quietly at your desk or on a bus!

Exercise 5 Psychic Flexibility (Group or Solo): Before doing this exercise you should build up your reserve of psychic energy with one of the preceding exercises.

In your relaxed but energized state, visualize a brilliant white cloud over your head just as in Exercise 4. When it is clear in your awareness, use the energy you have accumulated to lift yourself up into the cloud. Instead of the cloud coming down to you, experience yourself moving out of your body and rising to a place enveloped by the cloud. As you do this, take a deep breath and hold it for a slow count of twelve; as you slowly exhale, feel yourself slide back into your physical vehicle.

After a resting period, do it again, and then a third time. If you perform this sequence daily, after a month or two you will notice marked changes for the better—the details of the changes depend upon your personal needs. Your awareness will increase, and with it your psychic perceptiveness.

Exercise 6 Self-Healing (Group or Solo): Stand with your feet apart a bit wider than your shoulders, your head up and your arms outspread. Turn your left palm upward and your right palm downward. This is the Star position, immortalized in a famous drawing by Leonardo da Vinci, showing a man in this position within a circle.

Stand quietly and very still in star position and feel the life energy activating within you, at first in your left palm, then spreading. During this time strengthen your concept of life energies flowing through you; create affirmations and visualizations if you like, or just dwell on the thought of life energy flowing.

When you feel the energy flowing well, sit down and relax. As you continue to focus on the flow of energy through you, silently repeat affirmations like: "I am one with the universal life energies; they pour into me and through me now; I feel them. I am one with the universal life energy pouring into me and through me now. I feel these energies, I am one with them." Stay relaxed and let the energies pour through you for a few minutes.

With the flow of healing energy thus strengthened, focus your attention on any area of physical imbalance that you want to heal, and visualize the energy flowing to that place just as it naturally tends to. Don't push or try to make something happen, just witness the wonderful healing powers of nature in action.

Then formulate a desire for a reservoir of energy to be built up for your personal use. Your body knows where to store it, just issue a gentle command for it to be done. You can use this energy for healing, for psychic exercises or just ordinary activities. By doing this regularly you increase your capacity to store energy and draw on it quickly at need.

The next step is to visualize a golden aura around you, pure and bright. Let it grow into a pyramid shape with its point above your head. See this golden peak growing into a spire, higher and higher into the upper planes of consciousness, like an antenna reaching into outer space. This spire is an antenna. It is broadcasting your present need and desire to universal consciousness, and receiving the precise energies and awareness you need to realize them.

You should have an appropriate affirmation for this very special state. In this affirmation, request the strength and compassion of higher intelligence to help the growth, self-realization and self-actualization of yourself and everyone you contact. Affirm your desire that there be no harm to yourself or anyone else, and request protection and guidance. Put it into your own words, because your own words are always more effective, but request guidance in putting it clearly and appropriately.

When this is done with an authentic desire to connect with higher consciousnesses and to bring wisdom into service, you will feel an inner strength and peace.

13

Conclusion

For much of our lives we have had to rely on the authority of others—parents, teachers, ministers and priests. We held them responsible for our lives.

This book is designed to place you in the position of authority and responsibility over your own life. Developing your psychic skills will enable you to gather information from a wider source, and you will need to develop your discriminatory faculty to examine the information received, whether through your own abilities or through those of a psychic or medium.

Your faculty of discrimination is the ability to identify levels of meaning and their appropriate value in your life. Look for value, and if the information received has no value for you, do not accept it. The essence of meaning is content. Look to the words. Do they say something or are they meaningless babble? Make sure the words have depth and content and are appropriate to your life goals before accepting them.

Do not give others authority over you because of their titles, position, degrees or reputation. Those are the trappings that individuals use to assume the mantle of authority and exercise it to convert others to their way of thinking or believing. Look beyond the window-dressing to see if their words convey something of value and meaning for you.

You are the authority. Only you can finally reject or accept what you hear or see. If a person speaks on the basis of another's authority, ignore the source and listen carefully to what is actually being said. Does it have value or meaning? If not, you have nothing to gain by accepting it.

Words are the outer wrappings of content. Do not be deceived by pretty sounding words or sonorous phrases. They may be shallow and lack substance. The authority rests with you to decide the meaning and substance.

We seek authority in order to have power over others. Others seek positions of authority in order to have power over us. Real authority lies in taking responsibility for your own life and action, for everything you say, think and feel. Knowing that by your actions you are creating changes in your own life, present and future, you should also realize that you are affecting others. Your effect on others can be harmful or beneficial. It is your responsibility to make that choice.

What you send out will be returned to you in kind. Caring and consideration for others are values most of us prize as having high importance. If this kind of energy fills the thoughts we transmit, the essence of the thoughts returning to us will be caring and consideration.

The rule of no harm or hurt to others can aid you in your assessment of quality and meaning. If what comes your way carries hurt or harm for anyone, reject it. It is up to you to accept or reject all the ideas or energies presented to you. If you feel that what is presented does not enhance the quality of your life, then reject it. Anything you accept into your life should add to your happiness and well-being. No matter how well-meaning, intentions that create feelings of loss, inadequacy or unhappiness should be rejected.

We have spent time together in this book developing new skills which will make your life richer. Apply these newly learned skills beneficially to your own life and to the lives of others. Remember, life is a gift; use yours wisely. My wish for your success goes with you.

Bibliography

The American Dowser. The American Society of Dowsers, Danville, VT, 05828.

Bendit, Laurence J., and Phoebe D. Bendit. *The Transforming Mind*. Theosophical Publishing House, 1970.

Bennett, Colin. *Practical Time Travel*. Weiser, 1971.

Benson, Herbert. *The Relaxation Response*. Morrow, 1975.

Bloodworth, Venice. *Key to Yourself*. De Vorss, 1970.

Boone, J. Allen. *Kinship with All Life*. Harper & Row, 1976.

Brennan, J. H. *Five Keys to Past Lives*. Weiser, 1971.

Brown, Barbara B. *New Mind, New Body*. Harper & Row, 1974.

Butler, W. E. *How to Develop Clairvoyance*. Weiser, 1971.

Carrington, Hereward. *Your Psychic Powers*. Templestar, 1958.

Ebon, Martin. *Test Your ESP*. Wilshire, 1971.

Fiore, Edith. *You Have Been Here Before*. Ballantine, 1979.

Ford, Arthur. *Unknown But Known*. Harper & Row, 1969.

Glaskin, G. M. *Windows Of The Mind*. Dell, 1974.

Hills, Christopher, *Nuclear Evolution*. University of the Trees.

———. *Supersensonics*. University of the Trees.

Hoffman, Enid. *Huna, A Beginner's Guide*. Para Research, 1976.

Hollander, Bernard. *Hypnosis and Self-Hypnosis*. Wilshire, 1970.

Holloway, Gilbert. *ESP and Your Superconscious*. Best, 1966.

Keyes, Ken. *Handbook to Higher Consciousness*. Living Love Publications, 1975.

King, Serge. *Mana Physics*. Baraka, 1978.

Koestler, Arthur. *The Roots of Coincidence*. Random House, 1973.

Lawrence, Jodi. *Alpha Brain Waves*. Avon, 1972.

LeCron, Leslie. *Self-Hypnotism*. Prentice-Hall, 1971.

Lilly, John C. *Center of the Cyclone*. Julian, 1972.

Logan, Daniel. *The Anatomy of Prophecy*. Prentice-Hall, 1975.

Long, Max. *Psychometric Analysis*. De Vorss, 1959.

Maltz, Maxwell. *Psycho-Cybernetics*. Wilshire, 1960.

Mitchell, Edgar D. *Psychic Exploration*. Paragon, 1976.

Moore, Marcia. *Hypersentience* Crown, 1974.

Polansky, Joseph, and Greg, Nielsen. *Pendulum Power*. Weiser, 1977.

Ophiel. *The Art and Practice of Clairvoyance*. Weiser, 1971.

Osborn, Arthur W. *The Expansion of Awareness*. Theosophical Pub. House, 1967.

Ostrander, Sheila, and Lynn Schroeder. *Psychic Discoveries Behind the Iron Curtain*. Bantam, 1971.

Panati, Charles. *Supersenses*. New York Times Book. 1974.

Pearce, Joseph. *The Crack in the Cosmic Egg*. Pocketbooks, 1973.

———. *Exploring the Crack in the Cosmic Egg*. Pocketbooks, 1975.

Peterson, Severin A. *A Catalog of the Ways People Grow*. Ballantine, 1973.

Rajneesh, Bhagwan Shree. *Meditation*. Harper & Row, 1978.

Randall, John L. *Parapsychology and the Nature of Life*. Harper & Row, 1977.

Roberts, Jane. *The Seth Material.* Prentice-Hall, 1970.

———. *Seth Speaks.* Prentice-Hall, 1972.

———. *The Nature of Personal Reality.* Prentice-Hall, 1974.

———. *Psychic Politics.* Prentice-Hall, 1976.

———. *The Unknown Reality.* Prentice-Hall, 1977.

St. Clair, David. *How Your Psychic Powers Can Make You Rich.* Bantam, 1973.

Simmons, Charles M. *Your Subconscious Power.* Wilshire, 1965.

Sinclair, Upton. *Mental Radio.* Macmillan, 1930.

Steiger, Brad. *Secrets of Kahuna Magic.* Award, 1971.

Swygard, Diane, and William Swyard. *Awareness Techniques Series.* W. A. Reilly, 1979.

Vaughan, Alan. *Patterns of Prophesy.* Hawthorn, 1973.

Watson, Lyall. *Supernature.* Anchor, 1973.

Weed, Joseph J. *Wisdom of the Mystic Masters.* Prentice-Hall, 1968.

———. *Psychic Energy.* Prentice-Hall, 1970.

———. *Complete Guide to Oracle and Prophecy Methods.* Prentice-Hall, 1971.

White, Stewart. *The Unobstructed Universe.* E. P. Dutton, 1959.

———. *The Betty Book.* E. P. Dutton, 1977.

Resources

Dowser's Precision Supply Co. Pendulums
McCormick Building send $.25 for brochure
Trinidad, Colorado 81082

Venture Bookshop Pendulums, crystal balls
P. O. Box 249 planchettes, etc.
Highland Park, Illinois 60035

The American Research Team Recordings, cassettes
256 So. Robertson Boulevard to alter awareness through
Beverly Hills, California 90211 sound
send self-addressed, stamped
business size reply envelope

Potentials Unlimited "ESP Training Tapes
4808 Broadmoor S.E. free catalog
Grand Rapids, Michigan 49508

Unity Records free catalog
Box 12
Corte Madera, California 94925

Central Premonitions Registry To report precognitive dreams
P. O. Box 482
Times Square Station
New York, NY 10036

Center for Spiritual Emergencies For training in intervention
Big Sur, California 93920 in "Crisis" Psychic situations
408-667-2335

Index

HUNA: A Beginner's Guide

Revised Edition
Enid Hoffman

As author Enid Hoffman recalls, "I began to feel with rising excitement that I was on to something very valuable and real. I learned that this concept was at the bottom of all the practices of the Kahuna. Their miracles and magic were the result of their profound knowledge of energies and substances, visible and invisible. This knowledge enabled them to control their life experiences instead of having events control them, and made it possible for them to assist others to do so. I became aware that they were expert psychologists with a thorough understanding of human nature. Their understanding of interpersonal relationships and relationships between the selves and the physical world gave them incredible power.

"For me, these were very exciting realizations, holding the potential for everyone to grow in knowledge and power. My enthusiasm grew because I knew that if the Kahuna had done it, we could do it by studying the Huna concept, practicing their techniques until we were as skilled as they. Then we would be able to produce miracles, too."

Centuries ago, the Kahuna, the ancient Hawaiian miracle workers, discovered the fundamental pattern of energy-flow in the universe. Their secrets of psychic and intrapsychic communication, refined and enriched by modern scientific research, are now revealed in this practical, readable book. Learn to talk directly to your own unconscious selves and others. It could change your life.

ISBN 0-914918-03-6
220 pages, 6½" x 9¼", paper $14.95